THE ANATOMY OF PROSE

By the same author

THE ANATOMY OF POETRY

THE ANATOMY OF PROSE

by

MARJORIE BOULTON

M.A., B.Litt.

ROUTLEDGE & KEGAN PAUL LTD
Broadway House, 68–74 Carter Lane
London

First published in 1954
by Routledge & Kegan Paul Limited
Broadway House, 68–74 Carter Lane
London E.C.4
Printed in Great Britain
by Latimer, Trend & Co Limited
Plymouth

Second impression 1955

To

JOHN F. DANBY

and

GERTRUDE DANBY

with love

CONTENTS

INTRODUCTION

THIS is intended as a companion volume to *The Anatomy of Poetry*. I was driven to write *The Anatomy of Poetry* by the impossibility of finding an elementary book on poetry which should be what I wanted my students to read, or would wish people to read at school. In trying to write a similar volume on prose I soon realized that even if I ignored my personal prejudices I could prescribe no simple book on the study of prose. I could find nothing. Perhaps I have merely been unobservant; but if such books are infrequent enough to elude my enquiries for some thirteen years a new one seems unlikely to be superfluous.

Teaching, lecturing and marking examination papers have convinced me that though everyone reads prose most people are shockingly insensitive to it. Prose, though the most popular form of reading, especially as fiction, is more difficult to study critically than poetry, because the techniques are less definable and the concentration less intense. For the average student there is less to say about a prose passage; and it is difficult to find a prose passage short enough to be studied in an hour but having something of the unity of a lyric; these difficulties lead to the anomaly that a student with poor literary sensibility may, in an examination, gain more marks on a poetry question than on a prose question, simply because he or she, however immature, unimpressionable or even philistine, can at least learn how to make a fairly sensible technical analysis of a poem. Students often find it difficult to see that there *are* technical problems in prose writing, apart from the rules of grammar; moreover, they can apply no technical knowledge to the improvement of their own prose.

I have therefore tried to furnish some guidance to the elementary technical analysis of prose and to offer some distinctions and definitions that give the student the possibility of saying something and, more important, wondering about something. I have tried to give answers, however tentative and incomplete, to many questions that I have been asked at various times, in order that the thinking student may at least have a base from which to make further explorations. I have tried to hint at a difference between narcotics and nourishment, brains and tripe, without being more priggish or pedantic than I can help. I feel sure that a much better book on the subject could be written, but I hope this half loaf contains some nourishment.

I should have included more specimens of good modern prose had not the various problems attached to the use of copyright material sometimes been insuperable. I am much indebted to the following authors, executors, publishers and agents for their kind permission to reprint extracts from copyright material:

Mr. Leonard Woolf for a passage from Virginia Woolf, *To The Lighthouse*, and a passage from *Flush*, both published by the Hogarth Press.

Miss Rose Macaulay, Victor Gollancz Ltd. and Messrs. Curtis Brown Ltd. for two passages from *Personal Pleasures*.

Miss Stevie Smith for an extract from her *Novel on Yellow Paper*.

Gerald Duckworth and Co. Ltd. for a short passage from *Rose Acre Papers* by Edward Thomas.

Mr. Charles Duff for an extract from *Ordinary Cats*, published by Williams and Norgate.

Mr. Roy Jenkins and Turnstile Press, Ltd. for an extract from *New Fabian Essays*, edited by R. H. S. Crossman.

Introduction

Dr. G. E. Daniel and Penguin Books, Ltd. for a passage from *The Cambridge Murders*.

G. Bell and Sons, Ltd. for their very magnanimous permission to reprint with some criticisms a passage from F. Fraser Darling, *Island Years*.

David Stafford-Clark and Penguin Books, Ltd. for a passage from *Psychiatry Today*.

Mr. John Steinbeck, William Heinemann Ltd. and Messrs. Curtis Brown Ltd. for two passages from *Tortilla Flat*.

John Lane, The Bodley Head Ltd. for passages from *Ulysses* and *Finnegan's Wake*, by James Joyce, *Autobiography*, by Jawaharlal Nehru and *Works* by Max Beerbohm.

Victor Gollancz, Ltd. for a short extract from *We Who Teach* by Jacques Barzun and a longer extract from John Strachey's *Why you Should be a Socialist*.

Hollis and Carter, Ltd. for the lines from *The Hound of Heaven*, by Francis Thompson.

Mrs. Frieda Lawrence, Messrs. William Heinemann Ltd. and Pearn, Pollinger and Higham, Ltd. for an extract from D. H. Lawrence's essay *Reflections on the Death of a Porcupine* and four lines from his poem *Don'ts*.

Harper and Brothers, New York, for a passage from *The Rehabilitation of Speech*, by Robert West, Lou Kennedy, Anna Carr and Ollie L. Backus.

Mr. Nicholas Moore for some lines from his poem *The Return of William Shakespeare*.

Mrs. W. B. Yeats, Macmillan Ltd. and A. P. Watt and Son for a passage from W. B. Yeats, *The Unicorn from the Stars*, from *Collected Plays*.

Mr. Somerset Maugham, William Heinemann Ltd. and A. P. Watt and Son for a passage from *Catalina*.

Mr. Ernest Hemingway and Jonathan Cape, Ltd. for passages from *The First Forty-Nine Stories* and *A Farewell to Arms*.

Introduction

Miss Elizabeth Bowen and Jonathan Cape, Ltd. for one extract from *The Heat of the Day*.

The Trustees of the Mary Webb Estate and Jonathan Cape, Ltd. for one extract from *Precious Bane*.

I owe more personal thanks to Miss Margaret Owens for reading the first draft of this book and making many useful suggestions, and to Miss Moyra Carr for making further suggestions; I am also indebted to Miss Mary McGarrity for enlightening me about the pronunciation of Gaelic place-names. My Mother, Mrs. Evelyn Maud Boulton, who not only read the first draft and made many useful suggestions, but learned to type in order to help me to prepare MSS., has already done so much for me as to make all thanks inadequate; but I place this action of love upon record.

M. B.

Stoke-on-Trent
November 1953

I. THE GENERAL FORM
OF PROSE

Sir, at o word, thou shalt no lenger ryme.
Lat see wher thou canst tellen aught in geste,
Or telle in prose somwhat at the leste
In which ther be som mirthe or som doctryne.

CHAUCER: *Prologue to Melibeus*

I N examinations students are often asked to comment on
pieces of verse or prose. Poetry is usually more intense
than prose, often more subtle; many people who never
read poetry have a habit of prose reading; but it is probably
easier to learn to say at least something about a poem than to
learn to make intelligent comments on a prose style.

The difficulties are that prose looks easy and that the form
of poetry is very much more obvious than the form of prose.
We all speak prose, of a kind; all technically literate people
can write it, in a fashion; and it usually takes us some time
to realize that there are different prose styles. Even an illiterate
person could tell that poetry has some kind of formal pattern,
for the mere shape on the page would suggest this; and such
things as metre and rhyme-scheme can be defined by most
readers although they form only a very small part of the
definition of poetry. In my own experience as a lecturer and
examiner I have found that whereas most students are more
responsive to prose than to poetry until they have had a good
deal of help, and that they are more likely to read novels than
volumes of poetry in their spare time, in an examination or in

class they find it much easier to say *something* critical about a poem than about a prose passage. There is something to look for in a poem; some mechanical tests are possible; and methods of approach are known. Further evidence of our inarticulateness concerning prose style is found in the great difficulty most of us have in criticizing our own style in an essay, report or letter.

What are the differences between prose and verse that cause these difficulties?

First, the rhythm of verse depends on patterns of repetition, though without counterpoint this repetition would become tedious. In studying a poem we can find a basic metrical pattern. There may also be patterns of rhyme and sometimes other patterns such as assonance, internal rhyme or alliteration, refrains, symmetries of logic and even musical accompaniment. The rhythm of prose depends on variation. Indeed, metrical lines and rhymes are considered a fault in prose style.

Secondly, the function of words in prose is rather different. It would be very dangerous to make sweeping statements about this when 'poetry' includes Pope and Whitman and 'prose' includes Addison and James Joyce. But it may at least be said that it is rather more probable in poetry than in prose that words may be used ambiguously, evocatively, onomatopoeically or for a purpose connected with rhythm rather than meaning. Some of the most extreme examples of this will be found in Shakespeare, Wordsworth, Milton, Browning, T. S. Eliot and Dr. Edith Sitwell. In prose words are more likely to be sharply defined, with one meaning at a time[1] and with what might be called a utilitarian function. Clarity is a supreme virtue in prose for most purposes; in poetry it is usually a secondary virtue.

Thirdly, in close connection with this difference in the use

[1] C. K. Ogden and I. A. Richards: *The Meaning of Meaning* lays down a series of Canons for prose style of which this one is vital.

of words, poetry is generally much more figurative than prose, and, especially much more metaphorical.

The question of the greater emotional intensity of poetry is an even more difficult one; there is much quite readable 'nature poetry' of no great intensity, and there is plenty of prose, especially in drama, which may adequately express very strong emotion and have a very powerful impact on the emotions of the reader or hearer. However, the ordinary student of literature works mostly with the greatest poetry, and here it is fairly safe to say that the possible emotional impact is greater than that of prose.

It is perhaps unfortunate that by a natural extension of the meaning of the word, *prose* has come to have associations with tedium. We may legitimately speak of a prosy old man such as Polonius, a bad preacher prosing away for an hour, a prosaic problem or the prose of a monotonous existence. Prose is not inferior to poetry; the kinds are different. Forests are not inferior to oceans.

The units of poetry, with the exception of free verse, are the foot, the line, the verse, and then sometimes the larger section such as the book, canto, fytte or simply a section designated by a number or sub-heading. If we are to dissect prose we must take a different set of units: the *word*, then the *sentence* (which may itself, if a long one, be analysed into phrases and clauses), then the *paragraph* and finally the larger unit such as the *chapter* or sometimes a less defined section. The short story or essay may have no unit larger than the paragraph, or may be divisible into several sections where new arguments or matter are introduced; this will depend on the details of the nature or the piece.

If we study a piece of prose *word by word*, we shall be able to talk intelligently about the *choice of vocabulary*; if we then study it *sentence by sentence* we shall have a thorough grasp of its *rhythm, grammatical structure, naturalness, suitability to the subject* and *clarity*. If, then, we study the piece, if it is long enough, *paragraph by paragraph* we may find out something new about *rhythm* and shall understand the *logical sequence*, *narrative tension* or whatever else may be the general purpose of the passage. If we are studying a large piece of prose such as a whole novel we shall examine it *chapter by chapter* and so appreciate the whole *structure of the story*, or test the *coherence of the argument* in an informative or persuasive book.

We are not likely to go through every stage in this process. If we are making a commentary on a short piece of prose, in an examination, we shall probably spend most of our time considering words and sentences; on the other hand, no one who has a novel as a 'set book', or wishes to describe it for some other purpose, will be able to go over it word by word; here a more general analysis will be more profitable and practicable.

There is prose, such as some of Carlyle, Pater, Sir Thomas Browne or Virginia Woolf, that has some of the usual properties of poetry, other than metre, and there is some poetry, especially some free verse, which begins to approach prose at times; so we need some subsidiary categories such as *poetic prose* or *prose-poem* and *free verse*; but we should bear in mind that these terms are contradictions. In literature as in all the arts and most of the sciences there are many borderline cases and situations that do not fit formal definitions. The desire to fit literary works into over-formal definitions and classifications has given rise to much bad criticism.

The method of word-by-word, sentence-by-sentence and paragraph-by-paragraph will fit all prose, because it is impossible to have prose that does not consist of these units.[1]

---

[1] There may, of course, be prose passages in which there are no sentences in the strict grammatical sense, for it would be possible to write a paragraph consisting entirely of ejaculations or in the loose diction used to represent our actual thought, as in some of the work of James Joyce; but this is not common.

The General Form of Prose

It is also helpful to have in mind the idea that prose has a number of functions and that the function will, very largely, dictate the style, at least in a competent writer. We should therefore decide on the general function of a piece of prose when we study it, and cannot, indeed, say whether the vocabulary, rhythm and so on are suitable until we know the function. Very briefly, with some recklessness of generalization, we may divide prose into the following types according to function.

1. NARRATIVE

It seems likely that narrative prose is more popular than any other form of literature. It tells a story, true or invented in such a way as to make it interesting. This may be achieved in a variety of ways, from the mere accumulation of exciting incident as in a thriller to the subtle and detailed portrayal of character and motive as in *Madame Bovary*, *War and Peace* or *Pride and Prejudice*; thus the style may also vary over an enormous range of techniques.

2. ARGUMENTATIVE

This will generally be more abstract than narrative prose; here the adventure is intellectual. The function of argumentative prose is to persuade the reader to believe something. Examples are Locke's *Essay on Human Understanding*, Paley's *Evidences of Christianity*, John MacMurray's *Reason and Emotion* and most of the prefaces of Bernard Shaw. Good argumentative prose contains sound reasoning and may also include an appeal to emotion; much good argumentative prose aims not so much at convincing in the spirit of a propagandist as at making people think about the problem intelligently; this will be, or should be, true of most writing on philosophy and psychology. Argumentative prose may range from the very urbane and modest, as in Locke, Newman or Havelock Ellis, to the violent and dogmatic as in political editorials and election speeches.

3. DRAMATIC

A good deal of prose may be found in the drama. Important examples of entirely prose drama are the works of Congreve, Sheridan, Goldsmith, J. M. Synge,[1] Sean O'Casey, Ibsen, Strindberg, Terence Rattigan, J. B. Priestley and all modern commercial playwrights. Strictly realistic drama can be written only in prose. Dramatic prose usually has to resemble ordinary conversation sufficiently closely for us to accept it as an imitation of life, yet it must also have that improvement upon real life that is found in all art.

4. INFORMATIVE

There is much prose whose sole function is to communicate information; it includes: school and college textbooks, scientific books, encyclopaedias, books of instruction in various arts and crafts, reports of many kinds, and all those newspaper reports and articles that are not misinformative. Such prose may be of considerable literary merit, as are many history books, or they may be of no literary interest whatever but still satisfactory for conveying information. Some very bad prose is informative prose written by people who have no sense of style; this is understandable enough, for many people who have no interest in creating literature wish to convey information, and good style comes naturally to very few people. It is, however, stupid to look for a very ornamental style in a place where ornament would be a distraction.

5. CONTEMPLATIVE

Under this heading we may put the 'essay' as found in

[1] To the English ear at least, the prose of Synge and O'Casey frequently verges on the "prose-poem".

anthologies, some books of religious meditation, political speculation, or fantasy, and some books of descriptive writing, which do not conveniently come under more definite headings. People with a real sense of style may be able to write prose that it is a pleasure to read about such diverse and unpromising subjects as sausages, pebbles, mice, verbs or flying saucers. Famous essayists include Francis Bacon, William Hazlitt, Charles Lamb, R. L. Stevenson and Robert Lynd.

These five divisions give the main functions of prose writing. Occasionally a sentence is a unit in itself; it is then called a proverb or an epigram. Later we must also discuss the very important distinction between rhetorical prose and rational prose.

Here is a method of prose study which I myself found the best critical practice I have ever had. A brilliant and courageous teacher whose lessons I enjoyed when I was a sixth-former trained me to study prose and verse critically not by setting down my comments but almost entirely by writing imitations of the styles. Mere feeble imitation of the exact arrangement of words was not accepted; I had to produce passages that could be mistaken for the work of the author, that copied all the characteristics of the style but treated of some different subject. In order to do this at all it is necessary to make a very minute study of the style; I still think it was the best teaching I ever had. It has the added merit of giving an improved command of the English language and a greater variation in our own style.[1]

[1] Good parodies of verse are easier to find than good parodies of prose. The reader who wants to see some prose parodies will find some excellent ones in Sir John Squire's anthology, *Apes and Parrots*, and, often, in the competition pages of the *New Statesman*.

II. THE WORD

VOCABULARY

Costard: Now will I look to his remuneration. Remuneration!
O! that's the Latin word for three farthings: three
farthings, remuneration.

SHAKESPEARE: Love's Labour's Lost, Act III, Sc. 1.

THE choice of words is probably the aspect of prose style that is easiest to discuss. When we are studying a writer's choice of words, the questions that are of interest are: does he use, in general, everyday words or unusual words? does the Latin or the Saxon element predominate in his vocabulary? does he seem to use words consciously for their sound? does he seem to prefer the abstract, or the concrete word? has he any favourite words, his liking for which may perhaps be significant? is the general evidence pointing to slovenliness or fastidiousness in the choice of words? It may be an interesting proof of the importance of the choice of words in shaping an author's style, that a detailed examination of vocabulary, with regard especially to the frequency of certain words or kinds of word, has been used in the attempt to identify anonymous books, attributing them to authors whose other works are known.[1]

[1] The mathematics of this kind of investigation are explained by Mr. G. Udny Yule in *The Statistical Study of Literary Vocabulary*. This is a book for the advanced student only and also requires a considerable knowledge of mathematics.

The Word, Vocabulary

If we are asked in an examination to examine a short prose extract, perhaps two or three paragraphs, we cannot deduce very much about the habits of the author in his choice and handling of vocabulary, unless we already know something about his work. It is really unfair to generalize from one short quotation, though some reviewers imply that this can be done. In studying a brief passage we can point out rare or unexpected words; show where a word appears to be chosen for its sound effect; comment upon the rhetorical, unusual, archaic, facetious or figurative meaning of a word generally used in another way; notice such things as the evocative use of proper names or quotations, and so on; we should comment mostly on the vocabulary of this particular extract and not seek to generalize too freely about the whole work of the author.[1] On the other hand, if we are examining the whole work or a large part of the work of an author, as in a University examination or when studying a 'set book', we may fairly be expected to have some ideas about the general habits of this author in the choice of words.

English is a language in which the study of vocabulary is very rewarding. It is a great advantage to a language to have absorbed vocabulary from many languages, as ours has, for this gives a great range of shades of meaning. An account of the amazing cosmopolitanism of the English language may be found in any elementary book on philology, such as Jespersen's *Growth and Structure of the English Language* or Bradley's *The Making of English*. We have borrowed words not only from all the major European languages, but from—among others—Arabic, Hindustani, Malayan, Polynesian, the languages of the American Indians, of the Eskimos, the Australian aborigines and the Chinese. Many of these more surprising borrowings have been the names of exotic commodities; for

[1] Except in a 'context' question, where a short passage may be chosen because it illustrates some well-known characteristic of style.

9

the study of prose style, the important distinction is between the elements usually known as Latin and Saxon or Romance and Teutonic. For ordinary purposes of critical discussion, though never, of course, philological discussion, 'Latin' covers Latin, Greek, French and Italian borrowings and 'Saxon' the often earlier words from Old English and the Scandinavian and Germanic languages generally; 'Romance' and 'Teutonic' cover the same fields respectively.

It is not always true that 'Latin' words are long and unusual and 'Saxon' words short and everyday. *Street* and *cheese* come from the Latin; *maidenhood* and *holiness* are Saxon words. But in general the Latin word is likely to be the long word, the scientific term or the refined word, whereas Saxon words may be popular, short and sometimes crude. These two elements in our language have given us a large number of parallels—words with the same or nearly the same meaning, but rather different associations. Examples are:

SAXON, ETC.	LATIN, ETC.
speechlessness	aphonia
silent	taciturn
maiden	virgin
motherly	maternal
crowning	coronation
lawsuit	prosecution
thrill	vibration
often	frequently
feeling	emotion
under–	sub–
house	domicile
prayer	orison
deadly	fatal

Any intelligent student can find many other parallels by

studying an etymological dictionary. New words are still coming into the language; most new words will be 'Latin'—actually they are now usually Greek—because they are invented to name new inventions or other scientific discoveries; we already have words for most everyday objects. Examples of recent and needful coinages are: *psychiatry* ('Soul-healing'), *telekinesis* ('Movement at a distance'), *helicopter* ('Spiral wing') and *photomicrography* ('Light-small-writing').

The student who reads any books about words will not read far without realizing that there is a war always in progress between the Saxonists and the Latinists. Each side insists that the other side is very wrong indeed and gives horrible examples; but this war is rather like a war between men and women; neither can do without the support of the other for very long.

Some people have a passion for long words. To the half-educated, long words are a sign of education. We have only to think of the pretentiousness and the mistakes of Mrs. Malaprop. The morbid Latinist can never call a spade a spade; it must always be an agricultural implement. This kind of language is pompous and tiresome.

The Saxonists have something to say for themselves; but in a wholesome reaction against this clumsy pedantry they may fall into another pedantry and insist on using Saxon words when a word of Latin origin would be more suitable. It is a pity to be a fanatic on either side, for either fanaticism narrows the possibilities of language.

One habit all should avoid is that of using long words that are not understood. This fault is not likely to be found in the prose of reputable authors, but it may often be found in bad journalism and is a mistake that students themselves are liable to make. So many people talk loosely about *neurosis* and *complexes* and *repression* that the great healing and liberating science of psychiatry has suffered some discredit by them.

Aggravate is losing its accurate meaning and *atomic* is rapidly coming to mean, by association with the loosely-named atom bomb, something very big instead of very small. Slovenliness in language is the one real crime for any writer.

An aspect of the Latinist-Saxonist war is the continual campaign being waged by some critics against the use of technical language; some of them dismiss all technical language as 'jargon'. The very rich vocabulary of English makes it possible to choose words not only with regard to the meaning but also with some consideration of the sound and associations and the appropriateness to the context. If we take a noble passage of clear, simple prose and 'translate' it into the latinate diction of science, we shall see how a change of vocabulary can completely spoil the emotional force of a passage.

'Ah Sir Launcelot, said King Arthur, this day have I sore missed thee. Alas, that ever I was against thee, for now have I my death, whereof Sir Gawaine me warned in my dream. Then Sir Lucan took up the king the one part, and Sir Bedivere the other part, and in the lifting the king swooned, and Sir Lucan fell into a swoon with the lift, that the part of his guts fell out of his body, and therewith the noble knight's heart brast. And when the king awoke, he beheld Sir Lucan, how he lay foaming at the mouth, and part of his guts lay at his feet. Alas, said the king, this is to me a full heavy sight, to see this noble duke so die for my sake, for he would have holpen me that had more need of help than I. Alas, he would not complain him, his heart was so set to help me. Now Jesu have mercy on his soul.'

MALORY: *Morte Darthur*, XXI, 5

Anyone who knows English can understand this at once, though he may have to linger a moment over *brast* and *holpen*; now let us see what the fanatical Latinist would make of it:

The Word, Vocabulary

'His Majesty King Arthur acknowledged in an apostrophe to the absent Sir Launcelot that the deprivation of his assistance had been calamitous. He regretted that they had ever been in opposition, for as a result he had sustained a fatal injury of which he had had oneiromantic precognition. At this juncture Sir Lucan and Sir Bedivere attempted to co-operate in the transportation of the King; during this proceeding the King suffered from syncope, and Sir Lucan also lost consciousness, being so severely ruptured that a protrusion of his intestines was visible; simultaneously he expired from failure of cardiac compensation. When the King recovered consciousness and observed Sir Lucan, with extruded saliva in the region of his mouth and his intestines irrecoverably displaced, he expressed great regret that so honourable a nobleman should have succumbed in coming to his assistance. Sir Lucan had offered his assistance when himself in more urgent need of medical attention. His anxiety to be of assistance had excluded all personal preoccupations. The King added a benediction desiring the salvation of the deceased individual.'

Now, on dictionary definitions this means much the same; but it has lost all its beautiful rhythm, all its dignity and all its pathos because the vocabulary is hopelessly unsuited to the theme. This use of latinate, scientific or sometimes pseudo-scientific vocabulary to destroy emotional response to something can be deliberate; this is what makes the language of officialdom so detestable:

'During the recent aerial bombardment about forty persons sustained fatal injuries and there were some two hundred casualties with injuries sufficient to make hospitalization advisable. Most of the injured were persons not of the age to be productive or occupied solely in domestic duties.'

Try reporting the same fact in simple language:

'The recent air-raid wounded about forty people so badly

that now they are dead. About another two hundred have been hurt badly enough to be sent to hospital. Most of these people were either very young children or housewives.'

Any intelligent student can find real examples of stilted or technical language being used to disguise facts that would cause great indignation if expressed in more concrete language; the device is a favourite one with tyrants and also with people who wish to avoid responsibility.

We should not, however, conclude from this that whenever we meet something that sounds very technical we must despise it as being pompous and pretentious, or a hypocritical disguise. Technical language, however Latinate, has its proper place in genuinely technical works. Here is a passage of this kind:

'It goes without saying that there is always a reason for any of these departures from the norm; but the reason is not always structural, i.e. not always caused by structural defects of the larynx or of the resonators. Sometimes the disorder is rooted in neuropathology, sometimes in emotional disorders, sometimes in improper vocal habits. The voice defects mentioned above are the most typical of structural anomalies, though any of them may be the result of other causes. These non-structural causes—neuropathologies, emotional disturbances, and poor habits of vocalization—produce vocal effects considerably more diverse than those caused by structural conditions. (Dysphonias of the non-structural types are discussed in the appropriate places elsewhere in this text.) Before any vocal training is undertaken, the cause of the dysphonia should be ascertained, and in the search for this cause a laryngoscopic examination is the first step.'

WEST, KENNEDY, CARR AND BACKUS:
The Rehabilitation of Speech 1937

Certainly this is without literary beauty. The student who has understood the dangers of scientific language may for a moment feel that if this were translated into simple, everyday language, the result would be something as noble as Malory. Let us try cutting out all technical language:

'It goes without saying that there is always a reason for any of those things that are not like what is common; but the reason is not always the way we are put together, that is, not always caused by anything wrong with the shape of the voice-box or the parts from which the sounds bounce. Sometimes the bad speech is rooted in something wrong with the nerves, sometimes in upset feelings, sometimes in bad ways of talking. The voice faults mentioned up there are those we often find when there is something queer about the shape, though any of them may be the result of other causes. These causes that have nothing to do with shape—sick nerves, upset feelings, and poor habits of making sounds—cause kinds of sound much more varied than those caused by anything to do with shape. (Bad kinds of speech that are not to do with shape are talked about in the right places elsewhere in this book.) Before anything is done about teaching better speech, the cause of the bad speech should be found, and in the search for this a look at the parts with a tool that is meant to be used for this purpose is the first step.'

Is this really an improvement?

It sounds vague and childish; the rhythm is even less attractive than that of the original, which sounds reasonably brisk and business-like. There are now more serious weaknesses; the language of the original is clear to anyone who knows a few technical words or will take the trouble to consult a dictionary; but is something that is 'not like what is common' unfortunately abnormal, or something rare and precious? In what sense is the word 'nerves' used? it has at least two possible meanings. "Upset feelings' may last for a short time only; an 'emotional disorder' is a serious trouble that is with us for a long time. 'Bad ways of talking' might refer to ungrammatical talk, insulting talk or even to swearing! And surely no one will dispute that the word 'laryngoscope' means something much more definite than my clumsy paraphrase.

All technical terms have to be specially learned and some of them are a nuisance to bad spellers, but anyone who is going to specialize in some art, craft, science or trade will very soon find that to the everyday vocabulary a certain professional vocabulary must be added. Technical terms become jargon only when they are used in the wrong place to obscure the meaning or show superior knowledge.

Every educated person has some vocabulary that might be called semi-technical and that anyone is at liberty to use: such words as *incandescent, febrile, stamen, molecule, instinct, aqueous* are words of this kind. It is possible for a lazy student, perhaps more often a lazy older reader, to complain that a writer uses too many long words when the real fault lies with the reader, who knows too few words. Everyone who intends to read at all should possess a dictionary and know how to use it sensibly. We should also do what we can to discourage the spoiling of useful words by slovenly extensions of meaning. To be *allergic* to something does not mean to *dislike* it; *repression* is not simply having to do something we would rather not do; and no Hollywood release has ever been *colossal*. The habitual use of a word in the wrong sense at last kills it for use in its correct sense. How many useful words have now been spoilt by a taint of unseemliness because we are too shy to speak of water-closets and bellies?

In studying a piece of prose we should consider the exact shade of meaning of all the interesting words, and decide whether the writer has used the best word or only a word that will do. There is a difference that most people can feel between *grateful* and *thankful*, *manners* and *etiquette*, *ostentation* and *display*, *wealth* and *money*. Here are a few single sentences in which the choice of particular words is very happy:

'So that finding ourselves, in the midst of the greatest *wilderness* of waters in the world, without victual, we gave ourselves for lost men, and prepared for death.'

BACON: *The New Atlantis*

Wilderness is not only a suitable word to convey the picture of a great extent of water, with no food or land in sight; it contributes to the grace of the rhythm as *waste*, *space* or *desert* would not, its alliteration with *water* emphasizes it, it carries a faint flavour of the word *wild* and it has strong associations with moving episodes in the Bible.

'But if the Lord be angry, he needs no Trumpets to call in Armies, if he doe but *sibilare muscam*, *hisse* and *whisper* for the flye, and the Bee, there is nothing so little in his hand, as cannot *discomfort* thee, *discomfit* thee, *dissolve* and powr out, *attenuate* and *annihilate* the very *marrow* of thy soul.'

DONNE: *Fifty Sermons*, Sermon XX

'Whisper' by itself would do for an equivalent of *sibilare*, but Donne was a poet; he chose two words to increase the onomatopoeic effect. Then the long-drawn-out climax of disaster is made more powerful by the use of words of nearly similar sound; the last of these, *annihilate*, with its length, emphasis, and literal meaning of bringing to nothingness, is far more forceful in this context than *destroy*, *ruin* or *kill* would be. After this climax the crude, concrete word *marrow* suggests the grim realism so often to be found in Donne's sermons.

'Her head, *turreted* like that of Cybele, rises almost beyond the reach of sight.'

DE QUINCEY: *Levana and Our Ladies of Sorrow*

The Word, Vocabulary

Here a single word gives a vivid picture.

A great writer will never seek to impress by a mere display of rare or difficult words; but a great writer generally has a fairly large vocabulary, because great writers are interested in words and collect them, thus acquiring a store of words from which they can draw to express themselves more vividly than can the rest of us.[1]

John Milton was a classical scholar and had a very extensive latinate vocabulary, but here is an illustration of his power to choose now a rare word, now a common and almost colloquial word in order to gain exactly the effect he wants:

> 'I doubt not but ye shall have more ado to drive our dullest and laziest youth, our *stocks* and *stubs*, from the infinite desire of such a happy nurture, than we have now to *hale* and *drag* our choicest and fullest wits to that *asinine feast of sowthistles and brambles* which is commonly set before them as all the food and entertainment of their tenderest and most *docible* age. I call therefore a complete and generous education, that which fits a man to perform, justly, skilfully, and magnanimously all the offices, both private and public, of peace and war.'
>
> *On Education*

The firm, almost primitive monosyllables, *stocks* and *stubs*, *hale* and *drag*, are effective in giving a concrete picture and a sense that Milton is being homely and practical; the *asinine feast of sowthistles and brambles* is another picture, rich in associations and vividly concrete; *docible*, one of those rare words of which Milton was fond, is no mere pedantry; it means *teachable* but also, by its sound, includes the meaning *docile*.

While still examining a piece of prose word by word the reader should be looking also for slang words, which may be used for some special purpose, dialect words, coinages, foreign

---

[1] Great writers also occasionally coin words of their own.

18

words, puns, words used in order to startle or shock, words used to avoid shocking, quotations or disguised quotations, words carrying many associations, archaic words and Biblical words in good writers; in bad writers the student will also be looking for such defects of vocabulary as inaccurate words, slovenly uses of words and what Fowler's *Modern English Usage* calls Genteelisms, Vogue-Words and Sobriquets. So there is a good deal to be found out, and to be said, even about single words before we go on to consider how they are linked into sentences.

III. THE SENTENCE

GRAMMAR AND IDIOM

'And how did Garrick speak the soliloquy last night? Oh, against all
rule, my lord, most ungrammatically! betwixt the substantive and
the adjective, which should agree together in number, case and
gender, he made a breach thus—stopping as if the point wanted settl-
ing—and betwixt the nominative case, which your lordship knows
should govern the verb, he suspended his voice in the epilogue a
dozen times, three seconds and three-fifths by the stop-watch, my
lord, each time.—Admirable grammarian!—But in suspending his
voice—was the sense suspended likewise? did no expression of attitude or countenance fill up the chasm?—Was the eye silent? Did you
narrowly look?—I look'd only at the stop-watch, my lord.—Excellent observer. '

LAURENCE STERNE: *Tristram Shandy*.

WHEN a teacher looks at a piece of prose we have
written, the first question is, Is it grammatical?
There should be some other questions afterwards, though many teachers have not the time, and some
have not the ability, to ask them. When we are examining a
piece of printed prose we also may reasonably ask, Is it grammatical? It is not mere pedantry to take an interest in grammatical rules, for they help to form good style and, above all,
to avoid ambiguities. It is not impertinent to look for possible
grammatical errors even in the work of good writers; it is
easy to commit some not very obvious lapse in English,
which is a difficult language.

The Sentence, Grammar and Idiom

A distinction may be made between grammar and idiom. Grammar is a matter of rules, the etiquette of writing; grammar can be codified in textbooks and a rule of grammar, say, 'The subject and verb of a sentence must agree in person and number,' or 'No other noun may be placed between a relative pronoun and its intended antecedent,' is always true in the language to which it applies. (These two rules inevitably apply to most languages.) Idiom is less rigid and much harder to learn; it consists of an immense accumulation of verbal habits.

To say, or, still worse, to write: 'Has her goed out?', or 'We wasn't doing nothing!' are breaches of grammar. Most people do not show such ignorance; commoner mistakes are ambiguities such as: 'Hold the egg over a basin and crack it,' or the endearing mistake once made by a teacher of domestic science, 'Now take your liver, wipe it and cut it up.' While I was preparing this chapter I was confined to my room with a minor illness, and when a maid kindly brought my breakfast she said, 'I think the egg will be as you like them, it has been boiled with the students'.' In writing, an apostrophe makes the meaning clear; in speech, a disconcerting picture was conveyed!

Any intelligent person[1] can easily learn the rules of grammar in sufficient detail to avoid mistakes of this kind except as a rare lapse. Foreigners often speak English more grammatically than we do, because they have learned it as a foreign language, with rules; the foreigner is usually bewildered, not by grammar, but by idiom, which is unpredictable and completely irregular. The intelligent foreigner who knows some English never says, 'We was' or 'I wented'; it was possible to learn his verbs by diligent application; but he may say, 'I have a cup

[1] Except for the few unlucky people who are endowed with intelligence but with a curious incapacity to grasp anything verbal; these present a special educational problem.

and a saucer.' 'I have lost my hand-shoes.' 'I was very sorrow-ful to have caused you so much disconvenience.'—or, if he is trying to master the intricacies of English idiom, he may have even worse complications to face: 'I am afraid I have put my leg in it; I ought not to have let that cat out of the sack.'—'Is Madam in the house to me today?'—'I am sorry I committed a breach of promise to see you earlier, but I lost the bus.' These sentences are grammatically correct but idiomatically quite incorrect.

There are also some kinds of idiom which verge upon grammar; for example, in English the use of prepositions is very difficult to learn and cannot really be said to be governed by rules: we meet someone, have an encounter *with* them, or come *up to* them; we are in conflict *with*, fight *against*, are hostile *to* or *towards*; and to *set up* is the opposite of to *upset*; the natural languages are anything but logical in detail.[1]

In examining any sentence we must first ask ourselves if it is grammatical. In a good author, it usually is, though now and then a good author gives us a surprise. In examinations it is not usually necessary to comment in detail on the grammar of a piece of prose unless we are faced with a definitely gram-matical question; but a rapid check of the passage may be illuminating. We may notice that the author has linked a large number of clauses in one sentence with remarkable skill; that he is fond of parentheses; that he likes to repeat a proper name, instead of using a pronoun, for the sake of serious or some-

---

[1] It is possible for a created language to be without these irregu-larities, and still to be perfectly capable of life. A number of inter-national languages have been invented and these have a wholly logical grammar; they are almost entirely free from real idiom. These include Volapük, Esperanto, Ido, Novial, Occidental, Interlingue and Interglossa. At least the first three have been used with some success, and Esperanto now has a considerable literature that includes original poetry of merit.

times ironic emphasis; that he likes to use an active construction where someone else might have used a passive construction and been less forceful; that a scholar uses a surprising number of concessive clauses or that an uneducated man of action with something urgent to say uses short sentences. It may also be very interesting to notice how some authors who had a classical education use constructions more natural to Latin than to English—Milton sometimes does this—or, occasionally, how a style may show the influence of some other language that we happen to know.

The study of idiom may be even more illuminating. A foreigner almost always reveals himself sooner or later by some misuse of idiom or some importation of his own. English authors, however, reveal themselves by their idiomatic usage. Some writers never try to think of an original expression and seize every worn-out phrase that comes to mind:

'Mrs. Grey, who usually looks *as fit as a fiddle*, is rather *under the weather* at the moment. *The root of the matter*, for anyone who cares to *look into it*, is that a week ago *she trod on a stair that wasn't there*, *came a cropper*, *head over heels* and hurt herself *a good deal*. *As a matter of fact*, *she is doing as well as can be expected*, and *accidents will happen*; but she will not be *her usual self* for some days.'

These expressions were once bright and original, and 'trod on a stair that wasn't there' is quite a happy expression for a common accident; but a style that depends so much upon other people's ideas of expression sounds flabby and dull. Idioms that are worn-out become clichés.

Different kinds of idiomatic speech and writing will be found in different social circles and different professions. A university don might refer to a highly intelligent person as *an alpha plus*, a psychologist as *an I.Q. of 150*, a doctor as *bright plus plus plus*, an insurance agent as *first-class*, a jeweller as *a diamond of the first water* and so on. Many of these professional habits of phrase spread into the rest of society if they are often heard.[1] A highly individual writer such as Sterne, Lamb, Hemingway or Saroyan will have a highly individual idiom and we may find ourselves able to comment on some particular expression that is, in itself, a proof of some originality and individuality.

When we are studying a prose style, we find that grammar has its limitations as a guide to what is good. If we wish to write well ourselves, we had better write grammatically; but very good authors may use ungrammatical language, unidiomatic language and even very vulgar or slangy language in order to suggest the kind of person who is speaking. In a book of literary criticism, an informative work on science or a book of philosophical speculation, the writer will try to write in the most correct and dignified manner possible; he may sometimes go too far in this direction and become stilted; but in a novel or short story the author will be trying to make us believe in a number of people whose personalities differ; as personalities show themselves in speech habits, it will be necessary for even the most scholarly novelist to put some colloquialisms and even vulgarisms in the mouths of the less scholarly characters. Indeed, if the characters in a novel talk too elegantly it may be difficult to believe in either the reality of their talk or the sincerity of their emotions:

'The surgeons told him, that my Chevalier would not live over the day.

---

[1] Such expressions may be misunderstood. See Ch. II. One of my most charming linguistic memories is as follows: in front of a very intelligent person with little knowledge of psychology I referred admiringly to the I.Q. of a clever friend. A little later, my hearer, wishing to describe someone as remarkably stupid, said, "He must have a very low queue.' (I.Q. = intelligence quotient.)

When the Colonel took leave of him, Mr. Lovelace said, "You have well revenged the dear creature."

"I have, sir," said Mr. Morden; "and perhaps I shall be sorry that you called me to this work, while I was balancing whether to obey, or disobey, the dear angel."

"There is a fate in it!" replied my Chevalier—"A cursed fate!—Or this could not have been.—But be ye all witnesses, that I have provoked my destiny, and acknowledge that I fall by a man of honour."

"Sir,' said the Colonel, with the piety of a confessor (wringing Mr. Lovelace's hand), 'snatch these few fleeting moments, and commend yourself to God."'

SAMUEL RICHARDSON: *Clarissa*

This is almost embarrassing by its remoteness from natural speech—though it was probably a good deal nearer to common speech when it was written than it now seems to be. Nowadays it is usually in the trashiest literature, such as the bad historical novel, the scenario of a bad film or the cheap so-called romance, that we find the most 'literary' speech.

Much that would be crossed out by the teacher in a child's essay may be acceptable in a good writer because it gives an impression of naïveté, suggests the mind of a child or an uneducated person or conveys some special effect:

'Nick had swung on the freight train when it slowed down for the yards *outside of* Walton Junction. The train, with Nick on it, had passed through Kalkaska as it started to get dark. *Now he must be nearly to Mancelona. Three or four miles of swamp.* He stepped along the track, walking *so he kept* on the ballast between the ties, *the swamp* ghostly in the rising mist. His eye ached and he was hungry. He kept on *hiking*, putting the miles of track *back of him.* The swamp was all the same on both sides of the track.'

ERNEST HEMINGWAY: *In Our Time*

25

If this were part of a school 'composition' it might be lucky to gain 40 per cent. A teacher could justly write at the side 'Jerky' or the favourite 'awk.', cross out the *of* in *outside of*, write over the next italicized sentence: 'Is this Direct or Indirect Speech?' put 'Verb?' over the next sentence, insert a 'that' in *so he kept*, put 'slang' or 'colloquial' beside *hiking* and certainly 'slang' by *back of him*; a careful teacher might also try to explain that *the swamp ghostly in the rising mist* sounds as though it is in apposition, when it is not, and thus is awkward.

The artistic reason for this apparent carelessness is twofold. Mr. Hemingway is trying to suggest to us the experiences of an uneducated boy; and we do not think grammatically. This passage has some flavour of direct speech about it, although it is not so technically. Secondly, the sentence without a verb helps to concentrate the description and the short, almost clumsy sentences add to the feeling of anxiety and urgency.[1] Many other examples of ungrammatical style that has an artistic function will be found in the work of Mr. Hemingway. The reader should be warned, however, that the person who writes ungrammatically without knowing it seldom achieves this admirable directness and vigour; he is apt, rather, to flounder in long sentences, to obscure the meaning or to sound childish. It is likely that this could not be used as a literary device until several hundred years of literary experience had formed our ideas of a correct prose style; we cannot deviate interestingly from customs that are not themselves established.

It is generally bad practice for beginners to try to write long sentences; they usually become meandering and the

---

[1] This may sometimes also be true of the style of a child or untutored person who is sensitive. Miss M. Hourd in her *The Education of the Poetic Spirit* gives examples of happy accidents of this kind.

dependent clauses become entangled; yet the great prose writers of the seventeenth century, such as Donne, Burton and Browne, were fond of long sentences and achieved some of their wonderful variety and delicacy by techniques which the beginner may find treacherous. Here is Sir Thomas Browne beginning a sentence a little awkwardly, righting himself in mid-sentence and then sliding into a more graceful rhythm:

'Methinks there is no man bad, and the worst, best; that is, while they are kept within the circle of those qualities wherein they are good; there is no man's mind of so discordant and jarring a temper, to which a tunable disposition may not strike a harmony.'

Religio Medici

This sentence from a wonderfully sensitive modern author may seem to be on the clumsy side, with its double parenthesis; for the inexperienced writer to try to handle so much in one sentence would lead to stylistic shipwreck; but here the looseness of the style, combined with the rhythm, seems to stress the gentle irony:

'Just as an English peer who has lived a lifetime in the East and contracted some of the habits of the natives—rumour hints indeed that he has turned Moslem and had a son by a Chinese washerwoman—finds, when he takes his place at Court, that old friends are ready enough to overlook these aberrations and he is asked to Chatsworth, though no mention is made of his wife and it is taken for granted that he will join the family at prayers—so the pointers and setters of Wimpole Street welcomed Flush among them and overlooked the condition of his coat.'

VIRGINIA WOOLF: *Flush*

'All very artificial and unimportant,' these parentheses seem to

27

hint, 'these peers who break the conventions . . . oh, and these dogs, of course, too. . . .' Another effect of irony by construction is to be found here:

'I was always embarrased by the words, sacred, glorious, and sacrifice and the expression in vain. We heard them, sometimes standing in the rain almost out of earshot, so that only the shouted words came through, and had read them, on proclamations that were slapped up by billposters over other proclamations, now for a long time, and I had seen nothing sacred, and the things that were glorious had no glory and the sacrifices were like the stockyards of Chicago if nothing was done with the meat except to bury it.'

ERNEST HEMINGWAY: *A Farewell to Arms*

Here the long, awkward sentence and the rhythmical anti-climax after *Chicago* make the fatuity of war seem more obvious, even to the ear; the irony is harsher than in the previous extract. Thus when we are seeking to judge a style, though we should ask, 'How satisfactory is this grammatically?' we should also ask the more important question, 'At what particular emotional or intellectual effect is this aiming, and does it succeed? if so, by what technical means?' Indeed, this question might be said to sum up the whole of literary criticism.

For the sake of completeness it may be as well to comment briefly on the deliberate use of mis-spelling and bad grammar by characters in otherwise grammatical books as a comic device; we find this in Dickens, Smollett and many other novelists, ranging from these masters through the American humorist Artemus Ward, to the level of the comic strip. It may also, more rarely, be used for pathetic effect, as in Hazel's letter to Edward in Mary Webb's *Gone to Earth*. These tricks can easily be overdone by inferior writers. A particularly horrible example in a writer who could also create superb narrative prose is Kipling's *Thy Servant A Dog*, whose unreal baby-talk makes any sensitive reader squirm; and children's comics frequently treat vulgarisms and bad grammar as sources of fun, a practice which is rather unfair to readers who are still at school.

IV. THE SENTENCE

WRITTEN AND SPOKEN PROSE

Here lies Nolly Goldsmith, for shortness called Noll,
Who wrote like an angel, and talked like poor Poll.

DAVID GARRICK

ONE might think it would be easy enough to make a clear distinction between the written and the spoken, for the processes of wielding the pen and wagging the tongue overlap only in those very slow, semi-literate writers who find it helps to protrude the tongue when writing. Yet the distinction is not clear-cut. Oratory—the most literary and formal kind of public speaking—is certainly to be considered as spoken prose, for its original function is to be spoken on a particular occasion, and if it does not come naturally off the tongue it is worse than useless; yet many of the great orators extended their preparation of a speech to writing it down in full, and many of the great speeches of history have been printed for silent reading. All dramatic prose (except for stage-directions) must be regarded as spoken prose, but its style may be far removed from ordinary collo-quial speech, in the heightening that is one of the features of great art. The problem is further complicated nowadays by the fact that a short story may be written for silent reading but afterwards broadcast, or vice versa, that many modern authors like to dictate their work to a shorthand-typist or into a dictaphone and that, on the other hand, such forms of speech

30

as the important political statement, the sermon of general public interest and the lecture by an acknowledged expert are nowadays read, in books or newspapers, by far more people than can listen to them.

In considering the prose sentence from the point of view of grammar and idiom and, to a lesser extent, of vocabulary and rhythm, we must decide whether it is meant to be spoken, meant to be read silently, or, a subdivision of great importance in the novel, meant to be a representation of the speech of someone else.

We generally find it possible to use longer sentences in writing than in speaking, for the reader who fails to grasp a sentence at the first reading can turn back; it is safe to use very long and rare words in a piece of prose intended for private reading, such as Burton's *The Anatomy of Melancholy* or a scientific treatise, but someone writing for speech must confine himself to a vocabulary which the audience may be expected to understand at once. Poetry, more primitive and at the same time more exciting than prose, was a creation of people for whom only the spoken word existed, and all poetry should stand the test of being spoken (by a competent speaker, of course); but much prose was never intended to be read aloud and such a test would be unfair.[1] Thus, when examining a piece of prose, we should neither object to its bookishness if it was obviously not intended to be other than bookish, nor sneer at its want of formal correctness if it was intended to be a representation of common speech.

Everyone knows that many things are permitted in speech that are not considered good style in written prose: contractions such as *can't*, *won't*, *How d'y'do?* mild lapses from grammar such as 'It's me', inoffensive slang such as *right-o*, *O.K.*, *a little something*, *keep your hair on* and many idiomatic expres-

[1] To read our own prose aloud is, however, a good test of its fluency and clarity.

sions. There are also many expressions in which the tone of voice is so important that it is safer not to use them in a letter, though they may be quite harmless in speech: *you are an ass, I'm going to jump in the pond, come here and be killed!* Indeed, speech so fastidious as to renounce all the licences commonly accepted in speech may often be resented as 'talking like a book' or 'being superior'.

Any good novelist gives many examples of this differentiation. The descriptive and narrative passages will be written in the novelist's own style, which is usually correct and often highly decorative and individual; but when words are put into the mouths of the various characters they are made to speak much as they would speak in real life; whether they speak correctly or not, they must have a diction suitable to their character, education, environment, and personal preoccupations.

'The lady cried out fiercely, "Where's the pelisse!" meaning the constabulary—and she went on to say, shaking the handle of her umbrella at Tom, that but for them fellers never being in the way when they was wanted, she'd have given him in charge, she would.

" 'If they greased their whiskers less, and minded the duties which they're paid so heavy for, a little more," she observed, ' "no one needn't be drove mad by scrouding so!"

'She had been grievously knocked about, no doubt, for her bonnet was bent into the shape of a cocked hat. Being a fat little woman, too, she was in a state of great exhaustion and intense heat. Instead of pursuing the altercation, therefore, Tom civilly inquired which boat she wanted to go on board of?

' "I suppose," returned the lady, "as nobody but yourself can want to look at a steam package, without wanting to go a-boarding of it, can they? Booby!"

"'Which one do you want to look at, then?" said Tom. "We'll make room for you if we can. Don't be so ill-tempered."

"'No blessed creetur as ever I was with in trying times," returned the lady, somewhat softened, "'and they're a many in their numbers, ever brought it as a charge again myself that I was anythin' but mild and equal in my spirits. Never mind a-contradicting of me, if you seems to feel it does you good, ma'am, I often says, for well you know that Sairey may be trusted not to give it back again. But I will not denige that I am worrited and vexed this day, and with good reagion, Lord forbid!"

'By this time, Mrs. Gamp (for it was no other than that experienced practitioner) had, with Tom's assistance, squeezed and worked herself into a small corner between Ruth and the rail; where, after breathing very hard for some little time, and performing a short series of dangerous evolutions with her umbrella, she managed to establish herself pretty comfortably.'

CHARLES DICKENS: *Martin Chuzzlewit*

The fact that in a novel the conversation of the characters resembles, or should resemble, common speech appropriate to them, whereas the narrative portions may be in a much more elaborate style, may account in part for the preference shown by inexperienced readers for novels with a great deal of conversation.[1] This in turn may account in part for the success of, say, the commercial 'best-seller' as compared with the experimental novel which may be of immeasurably greater literary merit.

Letters, being normally prose addressed to one person, come midway between written and spoken prose. Business letters used often to be written in a hideous barbaric jargon of the 'Your esteemed favour of the 32nd ult. to hand and beg to

[1] Compare Lewis Carroll's *Alice*.

reply to same' variety, which, happily, seems to be dying out except where it has infected the ordinary letters of the semi-literate, who finds it impressive; but the personal letter closely resembles common speech; we feel we may be more loose in construction, and trivial in content[1] than in writing something for the general public.

Here is Byron writing a formal letter to his publisher John Murray and allowing his animated personality to spill over into a very lively postscript:

Venice, January 25, 1819.

'Dear Sir,

You will do me the favour to print privately (for private distribution) fifty copies of *Don Juan*. The list of men to whom I wish it to be presented, I will send hereafter. The other two poems had best be added to the collective edition: I do not approve of *their* being published separately. *Print Don Juan entire*, omitting, of course, the lines on Castlereagh, as I am not on the spot to meet him. I have a second Canto ready, which will be sent by and bye. By this post, I have written to Mr. Hobhouse, addressed to your care.

Yours very truly,
B.

'P.S. I have acquiesced in the request and representation; and having done so, it is idle to detail my arguments in favour of my own Self-love and 'Poeshie'; but I *protest*. If the poem has poetry, it would stand; if not, fall: the rest is 'leather and prunella', and has never yet affected any human production 'pro or con'. Dullness is the only annihilator in such cases. As to the Cant of the day, I despise it, as I have ever done all its

---

[1] Or a letter may be more emotionally intense than we should allow ourselves to be in public, for example, the love-letter or letter written in grief.

other finical fashions, which become you as paint became the Antient Britons. If you admit this prudery, you must omit half Ariosto, La Fontaine, Shakespeare, Beaumont, Fletcher, Massinger, Ford, all the Charles the Second writers; in short *something* of most who have written before Pope and are really worth reading, and most of Pope himself. *Read him—* most of you *don't*—but *do*—and I will forgive you; though the inevitable consequence would be that you would burn all I have ever written, and all your other wretched Claudians of the day (except Scott and Crabbe) into the bargain. I wrong Claudian, who *was* a *poet*, by naming him with such fellows; but he was the *ultimus Romanorum*, the tail of the Comet, and these persons are the tail of an old Gown cut into a waistcoat for Jackey; but being both *tails*, I have compared one with the other, though very unlike, like all Similies. I write in a passion and a Sirocco, and I was up till six this morning at the Carnival; but I *protest*, as I did in my former letter.'

The letters of Keats, Charles Lamb, Wordsworth, Gray, Frances Burney and Swift[1] are among others that are worth reading.

Another form of writing midway between written and spoken prose is the Diary.

Not only twentieth-century writers such as James Joyce, William Faulkner and Ernest Hemingway have sometimes adopted a style near to the colloquial in order to obtain special effects such as recording the supposed thoughts of simple people. Sterne was an early experimenter in this vein:

'I wish I could write a chapter upon sleep.

'A fitter occasion could never have presented itself, than what this moment offers, when all the curtains of the family are drawn—the candles put out—and no creature's eyes are

---

[1] Printed as the *Journal to Stella*.

open but a single one, for the other has been shut these twenty years, of my mother's nurse.

'It is a fine subject!

'And yet, as fine as it is, I would undertake to write a dozen chapters upon button-holes, both quicker and with more fame, than a single chapter upon this.

'Button-holes! there is something lively in the very idea of 'em—and trust me, when I get amongst 'em—You gentry with great beards—look as grave as you will—I'll make merry work with my button-holes—I shall have 'em all to myself— 'tis a maiden subject—I shall run foul of no man's wisdom or fine sayings in it.'

Tristram Shandy

This is the work of a very conscious stylist setting out to be colloquial; Charles Lamb sometimes seems, too, to be writing as he would talk. Here is a modern use of an imitation of ordinary speech to suggest the way we think, the slight inconsequence of thought and its comparative lack of grammar:

That was the last time I was ever abroad, and please help me that is the last time, it will remain so, so long I get this one fortnight holiday. It is too little for too much, to go abroad this way and back again so soon.

You are so tired when you come back. It is funny being like I am so tired, such a lot, it is funny, you can get a funny feeling out of it do you know. It is as if you weren't quite in focus maybe, it is like being a bit drunk, so you were lit up but still able to sit up and stand up and walk and smile, but it is there all the time, everything is shifted a bit the wrong way, like it was just a bit everything like G.K.C. says *the wrong shape*. But very funny, very funny-peculiar the whole way along.

It is funny how in that state anything might happen, and the most familiar things get a twist of the unordinary about them, like it was a dream. Oh how you pray to get the really ordinary, and the dream starts off. Well how's this, nothing to grumble about here. Why here's old Piccadilly and going along to Ridgways, and these people are just plum ordinary, *they might be real.*

They might be real. They might be real. I said they might— oh whoa up there, this is the password that let you right in on that anarchy of dreaming sleep.

'Oh there was an invalid for you—that fine writer de Quincey, that had all those purple passages I used to get by heart. That bit I said that he said, that anarchy of dreaming sleep, well now that is a purple patch. But when you're right in the middle of this anarchy then you don't care so much about purple patches, you don't think much of them, sniff, like cousin Joan in Egypt, you just don't think much of them.'

STEVIE SMITH: *Novel on Yellow Paper*

This kind of thing is more difficult to do well than it looks.

We do not really speak our thoughts any more than we write them, but it may perhaps be said that the type of prose sometimes known as 'the stream of thought' or 'the stream of consciousness' resembles speech rather than normal writing. This is prose written in an attempt to give a true impression of both the structure and the content of human thoughts—not in the intellectual sense in which thinking is distinguished from feeling[1] but in the more popular sense in which everything that goes on in our minds that we can perceive is a thought. Well done, it gives an impression of the chaos of human inner experience and the illogical sequences of thought, though in fact even this kind of prose has to select what is of most interest to the author. It sounds odd and perhaps ridiculous until the reader tries to listen to his own thoughts, when he usually

---

[1] We cannot *think*, in the sense of *reason*, without words; we can *feel* in mental images of various kinds.

finds that they are even more incoherent. This mode of writing might be called an extreme of realism.

The possibility of trying to represent thoughts in all their incoherence occurred to Oliver Wendell Holmes in the nineteenth century, but his method was to score it like a piece of music. He already recognizes the lack of grammar in thoughts:

'My thoughts flow in layers or strata, at least three deep. I follow a slow person's talk, and keep a perfectly clear undercurrent of my own beneath it. Under both runs obscurely a consciousness belonging to a third train of reflections, independent of the two others, I will try to write out a mental movement in three parts.

'*A*. First voice, or Mental Soprano,—thought follows a woman talking.

'*B*. Second voice, or Mental Baritone,—my running accompaniment.

'*C*. Third voice, or Mental Basso,—low grumble of an importunate, self-repeating idea.

'*A*. White lace, three skirts, looped with flowers, wreath of apple-blossoms, gold bracelets, diamond pin and ear-rings, the most delicious *berthe* you ever saw, white satin slippers—

'*B*. Deuce take her! What a fool she is! Hear her chatter! (Look out of window just here. Two pages and a half of description, if it were all written out, in one-tenth of a second.)—Go a-head, old lady! (Eye catches picture over fireplace.) There's that infernal family nose! Came over in the 'Mayflower', on the first old fool's face. Why don't they wear a ring in it?

'*C*. You'll be late at lecture—late at lecture—late—late —late.'

The Professor at the Breakfast-Table

The twentieth-century technique has a different effect; it can have not only psychological truth but fine, almost hypnotic rhythms at its best:

'He looked down at the boots he had blacked and polished. She had outlived him, lost her husband. More dead for her than for me. One must outlive the other. Wise men say. There are more women than men in the world. Condole with her. Your terrible loss. I hope you'll soon follow him. For Hindu widows only. She would marry another. Him? No. Yet who knows after? Widowhood not the thing since the old queen died. Drawn on a gun-carriage. Victoria and Albert. Frogmore memorial mourning. But in the end she put a few violets in her bonnet. Vain in her heart of hearts. All for a shadow. Consort not even a king. Her son was the substance. Something new to hope for not like the past she wanted back, waiting. It never comes, One must go first: alone, under the ground; and lie no more in her warm bed.'

JAMES JOYCE: *Ulysses*

If this is judged by the standards of the grammarian it is trash; but when it is taken as an expression of inner experience and read aloud the elegiac pathos becomes real and even dignified.

The danger of a very colloquial style or, sometimes, of the 'stream-of-consciousness', is that it may easily lapse into sentimentality or hysteria because it is not controlled, giving a rather cheap and unreal pathos to trivial ideas. The best of William Saroyan's work is great, but he can lapse in this way at times. Sometimes, too, a slangy colloquial style is used to give a false toughness; this may be found in certain inferior crime novels and thrillers, especially some American ones. Perhaps Mr. Hemingway occasionally slips into it when not at his best.

There is also a false dignity. Instead of erring on the side of the crude and colloquial, this is a style of pedantic refinement. It may disguise itself as Johnsonese—Johnson himself was a virile writer and always had something to say—or it may be a feeble imitation of the eighteenth-century antithetical manner; the very worst in this kind is a collection of the more respectable clichés and may be found in the leading articles of the inferior newspapers. It looks controlled, but a careful, critical reading shows its woolliness.

V. THE PARAGRAPH

Divide and rule.

LATIN PROVERB

IF there were no grammatical or stylistic reasons for paragraphs, it would still be necessary to have something of the kind. All readers know that it is easier to read a book written in relatively short paragraphs; a mass of type with no breaks is trying to the eyes. This is even more noticeable in reading manuscript.

We do not, however, indent merely where we think the eye of the reader needs a rest. This would be better than nothing, but might mean making breaks where the meaning demanded continuity, or vice versa. It might be said that while a single word expresses the smallest idea we can hold in the mind at one time, and a sentence is a complete thought in the intellectual sense, a paragraph is a small group of thoughts that hang together. A paragraph, though usually part of a story or other piece of prose, should make sense by itself.

'Fanny Elvington was a nice little girl, who had a great many good qualities, and like other little girls, a few faults, which had grown up like weeds under the neglect and mismanagement of the people at the Park, and threatened to require both time and pains to eradicate. For instance, she had a great many foolish antipathies and troublesome fears, some caught from the affectation of the housekeeper, some from the ignorance of the nurse. She shrieked at the sight of a mouse, squalled at a frog, was wellnigh ready to faint at an earwig, and quite as much afraid of a spider as if she had been a fly. She ran away from a quiet ox as if he had been a mad bull, and had such a horror of chimney-sweepers that she shrank her head under the bedclothes whenever she heard the deep cry of 'Sweep! sweep!' forerunning the old-clothes man and the milkman on a frosty morning, and could hardly be persuaded to look at them, poor creatures, dressed in their tawdry tinsel, and dancing round Jack-of-the-Green on May Day. But her favourite fear, her pet aversion, was a negro; especially a little black footboy who lived next door, and whom she never saw without shrinking and shuddering and turning pale.'

MARY RUSSELL MITFORD: Our Village

This paragraph is, in itself, a coherent description of a little girl's weakness; the next paragraph tells us how this footboy was always in her sight; the next goes on to tell how the boy tried to win Fanny's sympathy and the next gives a brief account of a conversation in which he tried to explain to her that their colour was the only difference between a white boy and a negro. Each paragraph treats of one aspect of the topic and each leads on to the next reasonably; this is the whole art of paragraphing from the point of view of logic. It is usually possible to find one sentence in each paragraph, called, in most books on grammar, the Key Sentence, which sums up the gist of the paragraph; in the above, for example, it is not the first sentence so much as 'For instance, she had a great many foolish antipathies and troublesome fears. . . .'

In normal paragraphing it is also usual to have the last sentence of one paragraph and the first sentence of the next linking the sense in some way. This is not an invariable rule, and people who in writing try to make it an invariable rule may find that they can never give the reader a surprise or divide a subject into a number of topics which are not very closely connected—as topics are not, always, in real life. How-

The Paragraph

ever, in any study of prose style we should give some attention to the linking of paragraphs. This linking will be noticeable chiefly in passages of description; in passages of dialogue the natural pattern of question and answer, remark and response, will carry the sense on without any more formal arrangement of the material.

'. . . A wound in the arm proved a disagreeable interruption to the poor fellow's meteorological observations, as well as to the tune of Nancy Dawson, which he was whistling. He returned the fire ineffectually, and his comrades, starting up at the alarm, advanced alertly towards the spot from which the first shot had issued. *The Highlander, after giving them a full view of his person, dived among the thickets, for his* ruse de guerre *had now perfectly succeeded.*

'*While the soldiers pursued the cause of their disturbance in one direction, Waverley, adopting the hint of his remaining attendant, made the best of his speed in that which his guide originally intended to pursue, and which now (the observation of the soldiers being drawn to a different quarter) was unobserved and unguarded.* When they had run about a quarter of a mile, the brow of a rising ground, which they had surmounted, concealed them from further risk of observation. They still heard, however, at a distance, the shouts of the soldiers as they hallooed to each other upon the heath, and they could also hear the distant roll of a drum beating to arms in the same direction. But these hostile sounds were now far in their rear, and died away upon the breeze *as they rapidly proceeded.*

'*When they had walked about half an hour,* still along open and waste ground of the same description, they came to the stump of an ancient oak, which, from its relics, appeared to have been at one time a tree of very large size. In an adjacent hollow they found several Highlanders, with a horse or two. They had not joined them above a few minutes, which

Waverley's attendants employed, in all probability, in communicating the cause of their delay (for the words 'Duncan Duroch' were often repeated), when Duncan himself appeared out of breath indeed, and with all the symptoms of having run for his life, but laughing, and in high spirits at the success of the stratagem by which he had baffled his pursuers. This indeed Waverley could easily conceive might be a matter of no great difficulty to the active mountaineer, who was perfectly acquainted with the ground, and traced his course with a firmness and confidence to which his pursuers must have been strangers. *The alarm which he excited seemed still to continue, for a dropping shot or two were heard at a great distance, which seemed to serve as an addition to the mirth of Duncan and his comrades.*

'*The mountaineer now resumed the arms with which he had entrusted our hero, giving him to understand that the dangers of the journey were happily surmounted.* Waverley was then mounted upon one of the horses, a change which the fatigue of the night and his recent illness rendered exceedingly acceptable. His portmanteau was placed on another pony, Duncan mounted a third, and they set forwards at a round pace, accompanied by their escort. No other incident marked the course of that night's journey, and at the dawn of morning *they attained the banks of a rapid river.* The country around was at once fertile and romantic. Steep banks of wood were broken by corn fields, which in this year presented an abundant harvest, already in a great measure cut down.

On the opposite bank of the river, and partly surrounded by a winding of its stream, stood a large and massive castle, the half-ruined turrets of which were already glittering in the first rays of the sun. . . .'

SIR WALTER SCOTT: *Waverley*

The italicized sentences or parts of sentences clearly form

links between the paragraphs so that the sense shall develop smoothly. The reader will notice how the last link does not come quite at the end and the beginning, though this variation in no way impedes the fluency of the passage.

When a completely new topic is introduced there may be no link between paragraphs; indeed, often, the more abrupt the transition is the more we are impressed by the surprise or have our attention drawn to an important item:

'Very well. I understand you perfectly, mademoiselle, and now I have only two or three words to say. This is the last week in July; in another month the vacation will commence. Have the goodness to avail yourself of the leisure it will afford you to look out for another English master. At the close of August I shall be under the necessity of resigning my post in your establishment.'

I did not wait for her comments on this announcement, but bowed and immediately withdrew.

That same evening, soon after dinner, a servant brought me a small packet. It was directed in a hand I knew, but had not hoped so soon to see again. Being in my own apartment and alone, there was nothing to prevent my immediately opening it. It contained four five-franc pieces, and a note in English.

CHARLOTTE BRONTË: *The Professor*

The 'small packet' is made more dramatic in its arrival by the lack of any introduction, any smooth gliding up to the topic.

Some writers use long, flowing paragraphs as a matter of general habit; here is a characteristically long paragraph from Coleridge.

'In this play and in this scene of it are also shown the springs of the vulgar in politics,—of that kind of politics which is inwoven with human nature. In his treatment of this subject, wherever it occurs, Shakespeare is quite peculiar. In other writers we find the particular opinions of the individual; in Massinger it is rank republicanism; in Beaumont and Fletcher even *jure divino* principles are carried to excess;—but Shakespeare never promulgates any party tenets. He is always the philosopher and the moralist, but at the same time with a profound veneration for all the established institutions of society, and for those classes which form the permanent elements of the state—especially never introducing a professional character, as such, otherwise than as respectable. If he must have any name, he should be styled a philosophical aristocrat, delighting in those hereditary institutions which have a tendency to bind one age to another, and in that distinction of ranks, of which, although few may be in possession, all enjoy the advantages. Hence, again, you will observe the good nature with which he seems always to make sport with the passions and follies of a mob, as with an irrational animal. He is never angry with it, but hugely content with holding up its absurdities to its face; and sometimes you may trace a tone of almost affectionate superiority, something like that in which a father speaks of the rogueries of his child. See the good-humoured way in which he describes Stephano passing from the most licentious freedom to absolute despotism over Trinculo and Caliban. The truth is, Shakespeare's characters are all *genera* intensely individualized; the results of meditation, of which observation supplied the drapery and the colours necessary to combine them with each other. He had virtually surveyed all the great component powers and impulses of human nature,—had seen that their different combinations and subordinations were in fact the individualizers of men, and showed how their harmony was produced by reciprocal disproportions of excess or deficiency. The language in which these truths are expressed was not drawn from any set fashion but from the profoundest depths of his moral being, and is therefore for all ages.'

COLERIDGE: *Notes on 'The Tempest'*

Such long paragraphs are difficult for the inexperienced reader and not suitable for some kinds of writing, though for Coleridge's inspired kind of philosophical criticism they are fitting; for a novel, at least when there is any kind of crisis or excitement, some shorter paragraphs are usual:

'I felt directly that Fanny's departure offered us a safe means of communication with London and with Limmeridge House, of which it might be very important to avail ourselves. Accordingly, I told her that she might expect to hear from her mistress or from me in the course of the evening, and that she might depend on our both doing all that lay in our power to help her, under the trial of leaving us for the present. Those words said, I shook hands with her and went upstairs.

'The door which led to Laura's room was the door of an ante-chamber opening on to the passage. When I tried it, it was bolted on the inside.

'I knocked, and the door was opened by the same heavy, overgrown housemaid whose lumpish insensibility had tried my patience so severely on the day when I found the wounded dog. I had, since that time, discovered that her name was Margaret Porcher, and that she was the most awkward, slatternly and obstinate servant in the house.

'On opening the door she instantly stepped out on to the threshold, and stood grinning at me in stolid silence.'

WILKIE COLLINS: *The Woman in White*

The short paragraph may sometimes, especially in contemplative prose, fall into single sentences, often of an aphoristic nature; this can hardly be called true paragraphing, but can be impressive. It may be caused partly by the influence of the Bible printed in verses.

The Paragraph

'He was of stature moderately tall; of a straight and equally proportioned body, to which all his words and actions gave an unexpressible addition of comeliness.

'The melancholy and pleasant humour were in him so contempered, that each gave advantage to the other, and made his company one of the delights of Mankind.

'His fancy was inimitably high, equalled only by his great wit; both being made useful by a commanding judgement.

'His aspect was cheerful, and such as gave a silent testimony of a clear knowing soul, and of a Conscience at peace with itself.

'His melting eye showed that he had a soft heart, full of noble compassion; of too brave a soul to offer injuries, and too much a *Christian* not to pardon them in others.'

IZAAK WALTON: Life of John Donne

The intelligent reader will notice that this could also quite well be printed as one continuous paragraph; and the Bible, when not printed as numbered verses, falls naturally into paragraphs much longer than single verses.[1]

Very short paragraphs may also be used for the sake of relief between long ones; indeed, good writers vary the length of paragraphs just as they vary the length of sentences, for monotony is the death of art.

So far we have given our attention to the logical structure of a paragraph and have seen that, whatever its length, it must have some unity of thought and will usually lead on to another paragraph by an obvious link. Another important aspect of style which cannot well be discussed until the reader has grasped the idea of the paragraph is rhythm.

[1] Some versions are printed in paragraphs.

VI. PROSE RHYTHM

> Still with unhurrying chase,
> And unperturbed pace,
> Deliberate speed, majestic instancy,
> Came on the following Feet,
> And a voice above their beat. . . .

FRANCIS THOMPSON: The Hound of Heaven

ONE of the differences between mediocre prose and great prose is that great prose has fine rhythm. The reader may perhaps be surprised at the association of rhythm with prose; is not rhythm one of the essential characteristics of poetry? Yes; but the rhythm of poetry consists, with a few exceptions already mentioned, of a regular pattern of stresses, varied so as to add interest but never so much as to obliterate the basic pattern; the rhythm of prose depends entirely on subtle variations.

Even before any detailed study of prose rhythm is made, it is possible to hear the differences of rhythm in passages with very different functions, all written, however, by masters of prose in one style or another, such as these:

1. 'The wilderness and the solitary place shall be glad for them; and the desert shall rejoice and blossom as the rose.

It shall blossom abundantly, and rejoice even with joy and singing: the glory of Lebanon shall be given unto it, the excellency of Carmel and Sharon; they shall see the glory of the Lord, and the excellency of our God.

'Strengthen ye the weak hands, and confirm the feeble knees.

'Say to them that are of a fearful heart, Be strong, fear not; behold, your God will come with vengeance, even God with a recompence; he will come and save you.

'Then shall the eyes of the blind be opened, and the ears of the deaf shall be unstopped:

'Then shall the lame man leap as a hart, and the tongue of the dumb sing: for in the wilderness shall waters break out, and streams in the desert.

'And the parched ground shall become a pool, and the thirsty land springs of water: in the habitation of dragons, where each lay, shall be grass, with reeds and rushes.

'And a highway shall be there, and a way, and it shall be called The way of holiness; the unclean shall not pass over it; but it shall be for those: the wayfaring men, though fools, shall not err therein.

'No lion shall be there, nor any ravenous beast shall go up thereon, it shall not be found there; but the redeemed shall walk there.

'And the ransomed of the Lord shall return, and come to Zion with songs, and everlasting joy upon their heads: they shall obtain joy and gladness, and sorrow and sighing shall flee away.'

Isaiah, Chapter 35. (Authorised Version)

'The world is a Sea, in many respects and assimilations. It is a Sea, as it is subject to stormes, and tempests; Every man (and every man is a world) feels that. And then, it is never the shallower for the calmnesse. The Sea is as deepe, there is as much water in the Sea, in a calme, as in a storme; we may be drowned in a calme and flattering fortune, in prosperity, as irrecoverably, as in a wrought Sea, in adversity; So the world is a Sea. It is a Sea, and it is bottomlesse to any line, which we can sound it with, and endlesse to any discovery that we can make of it. The purposes of the world, the ways of the world, exceed our consideration; But yet we are sure, the Sea hath a

bottome, and sure that it hath limits, that it cannot overpasse;
the power of the greatest in the world, the life of the happiest
in the world, cannot exceed those bounds, which God hath
placed for them; So the world is a Sea.'

JOHN DONNE: *Sermon LXXII* (1619)

'I have often been pleased to hear Disputes adjusted between
an Inhabitant of Japan and an Alderman of London, or to see
a Subject of the Great Mogul entering into a League with one
of the Czar of Muscovy. I am infinitely delighted in mixing
with these several Ministers of Commerce, as they are distinguished by their different Walks and different Languages:
Sometimes I am justled among a body of Armenians: Sometimes I am lost in a Crowd of Jews; and sometimes make one
in a Groupe of Dutch-men. I am a Dane, Swede or Frenchman
at different times; or rather fancy my self like the old Philosopher, who upon being asked what Countryman he was,
replied, That he was a Citizen of the World.'

ADDISON: *The Spectator* (1711-12)

'It must be a movement then, an actuality of the possible as
possible. Aristotle's phrase formed itself within the gabbled
verses and floated out into the studious silence of the library of
Saint Geneviève where he had read, sheltered from the sin of
Paris, night by night. By his elbow a delicate Siamese conned
a handbook of strategy. Fed and feeding brains about me;
under glowlamps, impaled, with faintly beating feelers: and
in my mind's darkness a sloth of the underworld, reluctant,
shy of brightness, shifting her dragon scaly folds. Thought is
the thought of thought. Tranquil brightness. The soul is in a
manner all that is: the soul is the form of forms. Tranquillity
sudden, vast, candescent: form of forms.'

JAMES JOYCE: *Ulysses* (1922)[1]

[1] First made available to the general public in England in 1937.

Prose Rhythm

'Senora Teresina Cortez and her eight children and her ancient mother lived in a pleasant cottage on the edge of the deep gulch that defines the southern frontier of Tortilla Flat. Teresina was a good figure of a mature woman, nearing thirty. Her mother, that ancient, dried, toothless one, relict of a past generation, was nearly fifty. It was long since anyone had remembered that her name was Angelica.

'During the week work was ready to this vieja's hand, for it was her duty to feed, punish, cajole, dress and bed down seven of the eight children. Teresina was busy with the eighth, and with making certain preparations for the ninth.

'On Sunday, however, the vieja, clad in black satin more ancient even than she, hatted in a grim and durable affair of black straw, on which were fastened two true cherries of enamelled plaster, threw duty to the wind and went firmly to church, where she sat as motionless as the saints in their niches. Once a month, in the afternoon, she went to confession. It would be interesting to know what sins she confessed, and where she found the leisure to commit them, for in Teresina's house there were creepers, crawlers, stumblers, shriekers, cat-killers, fallers-out-of-trees; and each one of these charges could be trusted to be ravenous every two hours.

'Is it any wonder that the vieja had a remote soul and nerves of steel? Any other kind would have gone screaming out of her body like little skyrockets.'

JOHN STEINBECK: *Tortilla Flat*, Chapter 13 (1935)

It does not take a very perceptive ear to notice that, for example, the Biblical passage suggests a need to continue by such light endings as 'desert', 'rushes', 'therein'—trochees—and the heavier endings 'walk there' and 'flee away'—spondee and amphibrach—give a feeling of finality and climax; that the steady beat of the mighty monosyllable 'Sea' in Donne heightens the emotional force of the repetition; and that this is strengthened by such contrasting polysyllables as 'assimilations', 'irrecoverably', 'consideration'; that the lists in Steinbeck's lighter prose suggest the accumulation of problems in the household and the final sentence of the passage suggests the kind of movement described, by its actual sound; or that the passage from James Joyce verges on a kind of prose poetry, or a mannered and intricate music of prose rhythm. Even 'lines' of poetic rhythm may be found:

> It must be a movement then. . . .
> (Cf. Shelley: 'I sang of the dancing stars . . .')
> Fed and feeding brains about me . . .
> (Trochaic tetrameter as found in *Hiawatha*)
> Shifting her dragon scaly folds . . .
> (Iambic tetrameter with one inversion)
> The soul is in a manner all that is.
> (A blank verse line.)

All these rhythms are suited to their contexts and are therefore good of their kind; it would be foolish to complain that Donne is not very sprightly or Steinbeck not majestic enough. Here is another passage from the same delightful book, in which Steinbeck works to a climax from an easy rhythm, half-colloquial, half a parody of the scholarly or legal manner, to a solemnity which is in part also a parody of the heroic manner; the change is handled very cleverly:

'What happened is attested by many witnesses, both men and women. And although their value as witnesses is sometimes attacked on the ground that they had drunk thirty gallons of wine and a keg of potato whisky, these people are sullenly sure of the major points. It took some weeks to get the story into line, some said one thing, some another. But gradually the account clarified into the reasonable form it now has and always will have.

'Danny, say the people of Tortilla Flat, had been rapidly changing his form. He had grown huge and terrible. His eyes flared like the headlights of an automobile. There was something fearsome about him. There he stood, in the room of his own house. He held the pine table-leg in his right hand, and even it had grown. Danny challenged the world.

' "Who will fight?" he cried. "Is there no-one left in the world who is not afraid?" The people were afraid; that table-leg, so hideous and so alive, had become a terror to them all. Danny swung it back and forth. The accordions wheezed to silence. The dancing stopped. The room grew chill and a silence seemed to roar in the air like an ocean.'

Tortilla Flat, Chapter 16

The mere attempt to read the passage aloud will show the difference in rhythmical character between the first paragraph and the second.

This kind of criticism, however, is vague; it is possible to analyse prose rhythm in detail as minute as the detail possible in the analysis of poetry. We shall, as already implied, be looking for something quite different; repetition and 'metre' are not wanted in prose, though lines of verse are sometimes found in rather stylized writers. Those in Joyce have been mentioned; Ruskin frequently has blank verse lines embedded in his prose, and there is a longish passage that is practically unrhymed verse near the end of Kingsley's *Westward Ho!* But these are not typical. Prose can be 'scanned', that is, divided into definable feet, by the simple process of marking the stressed syllables, and thus a complete 'rhythmical analysis'—never 'metrical analysis' of a piece of prose may be made. It is not difficult to sort out the feet once we have marked the stressed syllables; there will sometimes be minor differences of opinion, but this is equally true of the analysis of poetry.[1]

For the rest of this chapter I am very heavily indebted, as no student of prose can fail to be, to George Saintsbury's monumental book on the subject, *History of English Prose Rhythm*. Saintsbury was, however, hampered by a violent aversion to phoneticians, who have now come into their own, and therefore believed in 'long' and 'short' syllables in English. Few people can nowadays accept this. 'Grin' is certainly shorter than 'Green' if both words are pronounced with equal force; but if we contrast a furious 'And you just stand there and GRIN!' with a light 'A pound of greengages, please,' we see the variability of length according to emphasis; in English prosody what matters is *stress*. It is convenient to use the classical terms used by Saintsbury, but remembering that to a Greek or Roman they meant a pattern of short and long, whereas to an English prosodist they must mean a pattern of strong and weak stresses, or, more accurately, of stressed and unstressed syllables.

In English verse only four or perhaps five of the feet whose names we take from classical prosody are really necessary: iambic, trochaic, anapaestic, dactylic and perhaps the spondee. In prose, where the variation is greater, many more feet are found, and though there is little merit in knowing strings of technical terms it will be convenient to use them here for the sake of clarity. Here, then, are the names of all the possible feet used in English prose.

Two-syllable

Iambic	Unstressed-stressed.	('become')
Trochaic	Stressed-unstressed.	('golden')

[1] In my *The Anatomy of Poetry* I have explained prosody as to a reader who knows nothing at all to begin with; here I assume a little knowledge.

Spondee	Stressed-stressed.	('outcome')
Pyrrhic	Unstressed-unstressed.	('And so . . .')

Three-syllable

Anapaest	Unstressed-unstressed-stressed.	('catalogue')
Dactyl	Stressed-unstressed-unstressed.	('galloping')
Amphibrach	Unstressed-stressed-unstressed.	('intestines')
Bacchic	Stressed-stressed-unstressed.	('Margaret')
Anti-Bacchic	Unstressed-stressed-stressed.	
		('and bread sauce . . .')
Cretic	Stressed-unstressed-stressed	('eggs and ham')
Molossus	Stressed-stressed-stressed.	('Go! Scram! Out!')
Tribrach	Unstressed-unstressed-unstressed.	
		(and of the . . .')

Four-syllable

Antispast	Unstressed-stressed-stressed-unstressed.	
		('a cold chicken . . .')
Choriamb	Stressed-unstressed-unstressed-stressed.	
		('time for a sleep')
Di-iamb	unstressed-stressed-unstressed-stressed.	
		('a piece of steel')
Dispondee	Stressed-stressed-stressed-stressed.	
		('Eat, drink, love, die.')
Ditrochee	Stressed-unstressed-stressed-unstressed.	
		('Gather apples')
Epitrite	Unstressed-stressed-stressed-stressed or	
	Stressed-unstressed-stressed-stressed or	
	Stressed-stressed-unstressed-stressed or	
	Stressed-stressed-stressed-unstressed.	
Ionic *a majore*	Stressed-stressed-unstressed-unstressed.	
		('Jane fell over')
Ionic *a minore*	Unstressed-unstressed-stressed-stressed.	
		('Over went Jane')

Paeon	Stressed-unstressed-unstressed-unstressed or
	Unstressed-stressed-unstressed-unstressed or
	Unstressed-unstressed-stressed-unstressed or
	Unstressed-unstressed-unstressed-stressed.
Proceleusmatic	Unstressed-unstressed-unstressed-unstressed.

Five-syllable

Dochmiac	This term is used for any of the possible combinations of five syllables in a single unified foot. The reader who knows a little mathematics or is prepared to take pencil and paper and work them out will realize that these are numerous.

The intelligent student will probably have wondered what is the difference between, say, two pyrrhic feet and one proceleusmatic foot. At first sight it seems that the multiplication of terms is a waste of time and trouble; in English verse it would be; but in scanning English prose we often find that to split a four-syllable foot into two two-syllable feet is to make a break where there should certainly be no break. Nothing that is unnatural distortion of the patterns of normal competent speech can be correct scansion.

We are now qualified to take a few paragraphs of prose and make a full analysis of the scansion. This not often done in criticism and is not often necessary; but a great deal can be learned from it, not only about the detailed criticism of prose style but about good writing. The Bible contains some of the most beautiful prose rhythm ever created—but usually we must keep to the Authorised Version.[1]

[1] There are modern versions which may be more illuminating from the point of view of the *meaning*; unhappily I know of none that has the same evocative grandeur of phrase.

Lórd, thou / hast béen / our dwélling pláce / in áll /
generátions. /   1–5

Befóre / the moúntains / were broúght fórth, / or
éver / thou hadst fórmed / the eárth / and the wórld, /
éven / from éverlasting / to éverlasting, / thóu árt Gód. /   6–16

Thou túrnest mán / to destrúction; / and sáyest, /
Retúrn, / ye chíldren / of mén. /   17–22

For a thóusand / yeárs in / thý sight / are but / as
yésterday / when it is pást, / and as a wátch / in the
níght. /   23–30

Thou cárriest / them awáy / as with a flóod; / they
are as a sléep: / in the mórning / they are like gráss /
which gróweth up. /   31–38

In the mórning / it flóurisheth, / and gróweth úp; /
in the évening / it is cút dówn, / and wíthereth. /   39–44

For we are consúmed / by thine ánger, / and by thy
wráth / are we tróubled. /   45–48

Thou hast sét / our iníquities / before thée, / our
sécret síns / in the líght / of thy cóuntenance. /   49–54

For áll / our dáys / are pássed / awáy / in thy wráth; /
we spénd / our yéars / as a tále / that is tóld. /   55–63

Psalm 90, *verses* 1–9

My stresses will not, I think, be disputed much, though even
on this point some ears might object; many readers will
probably disagree with the division into feet at some point.
However, we can now see the contrast of stressed, mono-
syllabic endings and lighter endings, with the finality of the
stress at the end on a heavy monosyllable. We see how the
important words are also placed where, with their own strong
stresses, they are surrounded by weak stresses to make them
stronger by contrast. We may also notice, if we are beginners,
that the four-syllable and five-syllable feet are needed to describe
prose accurately. This short passage may be analysed thus:

1–5. Trochee, Iamb, Di-iamb, Iamb, Paeon.

6–16. Iamb, Amphibrach, Anti-Bacchic, Amphibrach, Ana-
      paest, Iamb, Iamb, Anapaest, Trochee, Dochmiac,
      Dochmiac, Molossus.

17–22. Di-iamb, Paeon, Amphibrach, Iamb, Amphibrach,
      Iamb.

23–30. Paeon, Trochee, Spondee, Pyrrhic, Paeon, Paeon.
      Paeon, Anapaest.

31–38. Paeon, Amphibrach, Paeon, Dochmiac, Paeon, Paeon,
      Paeon.

39–44. Paeon, Paeon, Di-iamb, Paeon, Ionic *a minore*, Paeon.

45–48. Dochmiac, Paeon, Paeon, Paeon.

49–54. Anapaest, Dochmiac, Anapaest, Di-iamb, Anapaest,
      Dochmiac.

55–63. Iamb, Iamb, Iamb, Iamb, Anapaest, Iamb, Iamb, Ana-
      paest, Anapaest.

We can see how subtle were the ears of the great translators
of the Authorised Version. In the first sentence 'rising' rhythm
predominates, with a note of exultation; one more iambic at
the end would have suggested a line of verse; the climax
followed by a rest of the final paeon avoids such an effect. In
the next sentence the two dochmiacs lead up to the tremendous molossus of affirmation; again the predominating rhythm
is rising. Then comes the portion about the weakness of man
and the shortness of life as compared with eternity. The
rhythm changes. There is a greater proportion of weak
stresses, mostly in faltering paeons. Though there is still a good
deal of rising rhythm it is less regular and confident. The
heavy spondee 'thy sight' makes a contrast to the faltering
account of human life. The 'flood' of God's power over life is
contrasted with the weakness of man who 'groweth up'. A
particularly subtle effect of rhythm occurs in the 48th foot,
where the very slight syllable *-ed*, barely pronounced, gives a

weak and tremulous conclusion; an anapaest here instead of a paeon would sound too confident.[1]

Then the rhythm changes to suit the change of mood. There is another falter of shame over 'iniquities' which, here, is a better word than the monosyllable 'sins' to suggest the tremblings of remorse.[2] Then we sweep into the great lines of rising rhythm and certainty, with the mighty final sentence composed entirely of iambics and anapaests. Four iambics in succession begin to feel like a line of verse, and the anapaest breaks this pattern; the last phrase is wonderfully firm, the repetition of anapaests giving rather the same sensation as some of the parallelisms of the *Book of Job* or the *Song of Solomon*.

Now we will examine in the same detail a piece of good modern light prose by a writer with an ear for rhythm, a craftsman who is also an artist. We shall not find rhythms like those of the Bible, but we shall again find rhythms appropriate to the emotional atmosphere and subject-matter.

They strút/and tríp/aroúnd us,/áll shápes,/all sízes,/   1–
all cólours,/all spécies/(for éven/a prétty/líttle bláck/   6–
cúrly-táiled/píg is at tímes/to be admíred,/and the ínfant/   11–
rhinóceros/has indúb/itable chárms)./We may enquíre/with   15–
Montaígne,/what this béauty/is thát/so pléases,/and whéther/   19–
it has exístence/outsíde/the indivídual/eyé and táste/; we   24–
knów/that it/has nót,/ and that this/in no degrée/dimínishes/   28–
its pówer/to rávish/and entíce./'The preéminence/in béauty,/   34–
which Pláto/ascríbeth/unto/the sphérical/fígure,/the   39–
Epicuréans/refér/the sáme/unto/the pyramídal/or squát. . . .'/   44–

[1] The *-ed* ending was sounded more definitely when the Authorized Version was made.

[2] The reader may like to compare the rhythmical effects of these synonyms in: 'Blessed are they whose iniquities are forgiven, and whose sins are covered. Blessed is the man to whom the Lord will not impute sin.'—Romans iv, 7-8.

Prose Rhythm

All the/bétter,/since Pláto/and the/Epicuréans/are thereby/   50–55
bóth pléased./I dóte/on that gazélle,/that táll,/líght-stépping   56–60
gírl/with her slánt eyés,/her smóoth/and hígh-héld héad,/   61–64
her bróad/and smíling móuth;/yóu on/that flúffy/kítten,/   65–69
that smáll/and dáinty/pérson,/with eyés/lárge and róund,/   70–74
clústering cúrls,/pínk róses/in her cheéks./As to that,/I   75–78
dóte/on her/also,/as on áll/prétty/créatures,/from the/   79–85
sáiling/gólden/eágle/to the gílded flý,/from the spléndid/   86–90
múscled/áthlete/to the/chúbby/bábe in báth./   91–95

ROSE MACAULAY: *Personal Pleasures*

Here, in reading, we should probably make even the heavy
stresses a good deal less heavy than those in the Bible; Miss
Macaulay seeks to please, to charm and to amuse rather than
to impress or move us. But once again analysis will show the
appropriateness of the rhythm. (It may be wise to mention
here that a quotation presents rather a special problem in this
type of analysis; the rhythm is there already, and the writer
can modify it only by omissions, not by changes. However,
the writer would probably reject a quotation whose rhythm
was completely unsuitable to the context.) Here is a tentative
analysis:

1–5. Iambic, Iambic, Amphibrach, Spondee, Bacchic.
6–10. Bacchic, Bacchic, Amphibrach, Amphibrach, Cretic.
11–14. Cretic, Choriamb, Paeon, Paeon.
15–18. Paeon, Anapaest, Paeon, Paeon.
19–23. Anapaest, Paeon, Trochee, Amphibrach, Amphibrach.
24–27. Dochmiac, Iamb, Dochmiac (with a slur), Cretic.
28–33. Iamb, Pyrrhic, Iamb, Tribrach, Paeon, Paeon.
34–38. Amphibrach, Amphibrach, Anapaest, Dochmiac, Amphibrach.
49–43. Amphibrach, Amphibrach, Pyrrhic, Paeon, Trochee.
44–49. Dochmiac (with slur), Iamb, Iamb, Pyrrhic, Dochmiac, Iambic.

50–55. Trochaic, Trochaic, Amphibrach, Pyrrhic, Dochmiac, Tribrach.

56–60. Spondee, Iamb, Paeon, Iamb.

61–64. Epitrite, Ionic *a minore*, Iamb, Epitrite.

65–69. Iambic, Di-iamb, Trochee, Amphibrach, Trochee.

70–74. Iambic, Amphibrach, Trochee, Iamb, Amphibrach.

75–78. Choriamb, Bacchic, Anapaest, Tribrach.

79–85. Spondee, Pyrrhic, Pyrrhic, Anapaest, Trochee, Trochee, Pyrrhic.

86–90. Trochee, Trochee, Trochee, Dochmiac, Paeon.

91–95. Trochee, Trochee, Pyrrhic, Cretic.

Most readers will at least agree on the two main rhythmical differences from the Biblical passage: Miss Macaulay makes a much greater use of three- and four-syllabled feet, with their lighter and less authoritative sound; and the predominance of the rising rhythm common in English verse, since English is a language of many monosyllables, is much more marked in the Psalm, in which there are few trochees. The rising rhythm is, in general, heavier and more serious in prose than the falling rhythm.

It is interesting to notice how in Miss Macaulay's musings we again find an increase in the proportion of iambics where the mood is more firm and confident, as in the passage 58–69, and how this time the paeon is used to suggest, not a penitent falter, but a light, pretended-scholarly, hesitation in 'and the infant rhinoceros has indubitable charms' or 'we know that it has not, and that this in no degree diminishes. . . .' The Cretic foot at the end of the paragraph surprises the ear agreeably with a very firm, controlled climax. The three Bacchics of 5–7 slow the rhythm where it needs to be almost ponderous; the reader will notice how, having attracted attention in the first sentence, the essay meanders happily into lighter feet and patches of falling rhythm to discard all pretence of solemnity.

A delightful sentence from the same book is to be found at the very end of the essay on *Disbelieving*. Normally an essay needs to end with some decision; most of the essays in this delightful collection, *Personal Pleasures*, end with stressed syllables, usually monosyllables. But for an essay on Disbelieving what could sound more incredulous than this?

I must/beware, thén,/of too wíde/and too déep/an in/credúlity,/and remémber/that there/are mány things/yet híd from us,/and that/réally/éverything/is extrémely/pecúliar./

This begins firmly, in the tone proper to a solemn resolution, with iambic, anti-bacchic and a couple of anapaests; but then the author tails off into the indecision of a person suddenly confronted with the oddity of the world. Two paeons follow a pyrrhic and are succeeded by pyrrhic, two more paeons and another pyrrhic, very weak feet; before the sentence falls completely to pieces a trochee, the high-pitched anxious word 'really' comes to strengthen it; then the last sentence of the essay actually finishes, we must not say concludes, with a dactyl, a paeon, and a second paeon in which two weak syllables are left hanging at the end. In many contexts this would be unpardonable; here it is brilliant.

In contrast to this a passage of imperfect rhythm may usefully be studied. My criticisms are of the rhythm only; the book has given me great enjoyment, is very readable and is in most respects very competent prose. Moreover, in a book which is scientific in tone a studied elegance is not so much in demand.

The géese/shed their flíght/féathers/in Julý,/and the/yoúng géese/are as yet/unáble/to fly./It is/a tíme/of póssible/dánger/ for the whóle/populátion,/máking it/nécessary/for them/ to repáir/to some pláce/of sáfety/for their/flíghtless périod./

    1–5
    6–12
    13–18
    19–23

The Súmmer Ísles/ráce of gréy lágs/are fórtunate/in háving/ 24-
the íslet/of Ghlas Léac Béag¹/as a retréat./This pláce/ 28-
líes a míle/to the nórth/of Clerách,/and excépt/for very 32-
few dáys/of the yéar/is inaccéssible/to húman béings./ 36-
The swéll thére/will be hígh/when éverything else/is flát 40-
cálm,/and as the/lánding-place/is a róck/which shélves/into 43-
the séa,/it is álways/dángerous/to take chánces/with a bóat./ 48-
One móment/you may be afloát/and the néxt/find the 53-
boát/lying dry/on the róck/and yoursélf/tipped oút./The 56-
hérbage/of Ghlas Leác/is gréen/and súcculent/and kéeps 61-
the geése/throughóut/Aúgust./Práctically/the whóle/ 65-
populátion/is gáthered thére/by that tíme/and feéds/in péace/ 70-
until/the néw/flíght feáthers/have cóme./If sómeone doés/ 75-
distúrb them/and is so crúel/as to try/to rún them dówn,/ 80-
the bírds/have a sécond/liné of defénce./They quíckly/táke 84-
to the wáter,/scátter and divé./Cértainly/they cánnot 88-
stáy/under/for very lóng,/but their móvements/are súdden/ 91-
and béyond/prognóstication./ 96-

F. FRASER DARLING: *Island Years*, p. 70

Though this is not bad prose from some points of view, we
miss the delicacy of rhythm in the passages previously studied.
It appears to be the product of an untrained, though uncor-
rupted, ear. Here is a tentative analysis.

1–5. Iamb, Anapaest, Trochee, Anapaest, Pyrrhic.
6–13. Spondee, Tribrach, Amphibrach, Pyrrhic, Pyrrhic,
Iamb, Paeon, Trochee.
14–18. Anapaest, Paeon, Dactyl, Paeon, Pyrrhic.
19–23. Anapaest, Anapaest, Amphibrach, Pyrrhic, Ditrochee.
24–27. Di-iamb, Epitrite, Paeon, Amphibrach.
28–31. Amphibrach, Ionic *a minore*, Paeon, Iamb.
32–35. Cretic, Anapaest, Anapaest, Anapaest.

¹ A Gaelic-speaking student kindly assures me that these are monosyllables.

36–39. Dochmiac, Anapaest, Dochmiac, Di-iamb (slurred).
40–42. Anti-Bacchic, Anapaest, Dochmiac.
43–47. Anti-Bacchic, Tribrach, Dactyl, Anapaest, Iamb.
48–52. Paeon, Paeon, Dactyl, Paeon, Anapaest.
53–55. Amphibrach, Dochmiac, Anapaest.
56–60. Anapaest, Anapaest, Anapaest, Iambic, Anapaest.
61–64. Amphibrach, Anapaest, Iamb, Paeon.
65–69. Di-iamb, Iamb, Trochee, Paeon, Iamb.
70–74. Paeon, Di-iamb, Anapaest, Iamb, Iamb.
75–79. Pyrrhic, Pyrrhic, Bacchic, Iamb, Di-iamb.
80–83. Amphibrach, Dochmiac, Anapaest, Di-iamb.
84–87. Iamb, Paeon, Choriamb, Amphibrach.
88–90. Dochmiac, Choriamb, Dactyl.
91–95. Di-iamb, Pyrrhic, Paeon, Paeon, Amphibrach.
96–97. Anapaest, Dochmiac.

What makes this passage rhythmically less satisfying than the others? First, the rhyme at the beginning is unfortunate, and is emphasized by the fact that the stress is each time on the rhyming syllable. In English it is distressingly easy to put a rhyme or a jingle where we do not want it. There are probably too many trisyllabic feet in the passage; the run of anapaests in 52–60 is particularly sing-song. The paeon is invaluable for faltering in mid-sentence or working up to a climax, but if there is no climax, no stronger foot to follow, it is apt to give an impression of weakness. One sentence here ends with a paeon; and though the dochmiac foot is capable of some of the most powerful dramatic effects in prose, it was surely a mistake to end a paragraph with so indefinite a dochmiac. This is, of course, a harsh, hypercritical analysis; but it serves to show the difference between competence and artistry.

This kind of very close analysis of prose rhythms is not recommended as a habitual exercise, any more than it is desirable always to scan a poem when we read it; tables and technical language are no substitute for the ear as guides to what is best in prose; and rhythm is not the whole of artistry in prose. However, such exercises help to sharpen the critical ear. Here are a few further passages worthy of analysis; they are chosen from different periods.

'And when Sir Ector heard such noise and light in the quire of Joyous Gard, he alight and put his horse from him, and came into the quire, and there he saw men sing and weep. And all they knew Sir Ector, but he knew not them. Then went Sir Bors unto Sir Ector, and told him how there lay his brother Sir Lancelot dead. And then Sir Ector threw his shield, sword and helm from him; and when he beheld Sir Lancelot's visage he fell down in a swoon. And when he awaked it were hard for any tongue to tell the doleful complaints he made for his brother. Ah, Lancelot, he said, thou were head of all christian knights; and now I dare say, said Sir Ector, thou Sir Lancelot, there thou liest, that thou wert never matched of earthly knight's hand; and thou wert the courtiest knight that ever bare shield; and thou wert the truest friend to thy lover that ever bestrode horse; and thou wert the truest lover of a sinful man that ever loved woman; and thou wert the kindest man that ever strake with sword; and thou wert the goodliest person ever came among press of knights; and thou wast the meekest man and the gentlest that ever ate in hall among ladies; and thou were the sternest knight to thy mortal foe that ever put spear in the rest.'

SIR THOMAS MALORY: *Morte D'arthur*, XXI, 13

'The character of his mind is an utter want of independence and magnanimity in all that he attempts. He cannot go alone; he must have crutches, a go-cart and trammels, or he is timid, fretful and helpless as a child. He cannot conceive of anything different from what he finds it, and hates those who pretend to a greater reach of intellect or boldness of spirit than him-

self. He inclines, by a natural and deliberate bias, to the traditional in laws and government, to the orthodox in religion, to
the safe in opinion, to the trite in imagination, to the technical
in style, to whatever implies a surrender of individual judgment into the hands of authority and a subjection of individual
feeling to mechanic rules.'

WILLIM HAZLITT: *The Spirit of the Age.* (On Gifford)

'And Timsy, the cat, as she spies on the chipmunks, crouches
in another sort of oblivion, soft, and still. The chipmunks come
to drink the milk from the chicken's bowl. Two of them met
at the bowl. They were little squirrely things with stripes
down their backs. They sat up in front of one another, lifting
their inquisitive little noses and humping their backs. Then
each put its two little hands on the other's shoulders, they
reared up, gazing into each other's faces; and finally they put
their two little noses together, in a sort of a kiss.

'But Miss Timsy can't stand this. In a soft, white-and-
yellow leap she is after them. They skip with the darting jerk
of chipmunks, to the wood-heap, and with one soft, high-
leaping sideways bound Timsy goes through the air. Her
snowflake of a paw comes down on one of the chipmunks.
She looks at it for a second. It squirms. Swiftly and trium-
phantly she puts her two flowery little white paws on it, legs
straight out in front of her, back arched, gazing concen-
tratedly yet whimsically. Chipmunk does not stir. She takes it
softly in her mouth, where it dangles softly, like a lady's
tippet. And with a proud prancing motion the Timsy sets off
towards the house, her white little feet hardly touching the
ground.'

D. H. LAWRENCE:
Reflections on the Death of a Porcupine (an essay)

There are some special kinds of prose rhythm which are, to
an English ear, unexpected. These include the English versions

of the poems of Rabindranath Tagore and the Irish-English prose of Sean O'Casey, J. M. Synge and W. B. Yeats in their plays:

'Maybe so, maybe so. It seems to me yesterday his cheeks were bloomy all the while, and now he is as pale as wood ashes. Sure, we must all come to it at the last. Well, my white-headed darling, it is you were the bush among us all, and you to be cut down in your prime. Gentle and simple, everyone liked you. It is no narrow heart you had, it is you were for spending and not for getting. It is you made a good wake for yourself, scattering your estate in one night only in beer and wine for the whole province; and that you may be sitting in the middle of Paradise and in the chair of the Braces!

W. B. YEATS: *The Unicorn from the Stars* (Act III)

There is more of a lilt in this than we find in the conversational speech of English people. There is also a characteristic Welsh lilt that may be found in the prose of Dylan Thomas or the plays of Thomas Hughes.

Discussion of stresses and feet is for the student, the analyst who is trying to be objective. Let it not be thought that the translators of the Bible, or any lesser writers of good prose with a grand rhythm, sat down to a half-finished paragraph and said, 'I think it is time I had a dochmiac here to lighten the line, or it will be heavy; but I must end with a stressed mono-syllable or it will not be definite enough. I do not like those four anapaests coming together; I must change one of them.' It is difficult to know how the good writer acquires the habit of good rhythm. Certainly he will be conscious of rhythm.

It is, however, probably that the rhythms of the Authorised Version, Donne's Sermons, Sir Thomas Browne, D. H. Lawrence or any other great creators of individual and memorable prose were dictated by some kind of inner pres-sure, hardly felt at the time, just as the rhythms of poetry seem to come into the head almost unbidden. Possibly these things bear some relationship to the physical sensations associated with strong emotion—the rate of breathing, the heartbeat, the frantic, eager or apathetic movements of the body. Certainly they are not worked out step by step with conscious artifice; only the final polishing, the removal of lapses, is a conscious process. When we try to enquire into these larger problems of the whole nature of artistic creation, the trouble is that the mind of the artist, during this process, is far too busy with the immediate urge to be watching what happens. Thus all our knowledge of such processes is fragmentary, a collection of shining scraps.

VII. INDIVIDUAL AND COMMON STYLE

He speakes no language; if strange meats displease,
Art can deceive, or hunger force my tast,
But Pedants motley tongue, souldiers bumbast,
Mountebankes drugtongue, nor the termes of law
Are strong enough preparatives, to draw
Me to beare this.

JOHN DONNE: Satyr IIII

THERE are many possible classifications of types of prose style, and more will be said about these in subsequent chapters; but it is convenient to begin with the most general distinction possible, that between individual and common style.

Here are four paragraphs from four modern books, none being literary masterpieces but none being in any way discreditable to the author:

'You are at present reading this book. You have, I hope, your attention fixed upon what I am trying to convey; at the same time you are perhaps aware, although less acutely, of the position in which you are stitting or standing, and of a number of other immediate mental or physical factors in your present existence. All these are to some extent present in consciousness. Think now for a moment of the date of your birthday, or of a few words of a foreign language which you may know, or of any of the innumerable facts or fancies in your life which were not present in consciousness when you began to read this sentence. Thus summoned, they are immediately present. They have entered consciousness from another part of your mind where they were held immediately available but quite unobtrusive. We can call this much larger area of your mind, wherein much of what you remember is stored available for immediate recall when wanted, the pre-conscious area.'

DAVID STAFFORD-CLARK: *Psychiatry Today*

'Therefore, recognising that it is the duty of socialists to press as hard as they can for an ever greater degree of equality, but accepting the fact that such delays as will occur should not, for the reasons just given, be treated with too much intolerance, we can turn to the methods of advance.

'First, we have the methods which have been used in the past. The recent move towards equality can be largely accounted for under the two heads of the change from mass unemployment to full employment and of the use of heavy taxation upon the rich to finance a greatly extended structure of social services. The former change has not only enabled a great number of persons who were previously below the poverty level to earn a reasonable wage; it has also substantially improved the bargaining position of the working class, and therefore the pre-tax share of the national income which its members have been able to obtain. But it is not a weapon which remains sharp for use. Transition towards full employment cannot be a continuous process.'

ROY JENKINS in *New Fabian Essays*

'June Westmacott was away a few minutes, and then came back with the letter. 'Here it is', she said, handing it to the Superintendent. His heart gave a sudden quick beat when he saw that the letter was in its original envelope. The franking mark was blurred over the stamp, but the last three letters 'DGE' of Cambridge were visible, and also the date. The

Superintendent smiled when he saw it. It was quite clearly March 11th. If Briggs' description of the Cambridge postal system was correct, then the letter was posted after eleven o'clock, without any doubt, which fitted in with the time of its receipt. It was clear that Fothergill must be interviewed as remorselessly and as quickly as possible. The Superintendent read through the letter quickly and gave it back to the girl. It was a very sentimental letter, and it all fitted in with the notion of having been written, as Fothergill said in his second statement, late on the Monday night.'

DILWYN REES: *The Cambridge Murders*

'Nobody who has ever passed a moment in contemplating cats can have failed to think of and marvel at their remarkable ability as survivalists however difficult the circumstances. This is acknowledged in the popular saying that a cat has 'nine lives', and it is usually dismissed as due to the cat's 'nature'. Such an explanation is not good enough. I see it in this way. In the whole of nature the cat is the only animal which has solved the problem of living in close contact with human beings and at the same time of maintaining its freedom and conserving its own personality. This truth we must acknowledge. Empires and systems may come and go, tyrants may rule with their rods of iron or steel, they may bend men to their wills or turn them into complacent slaves. The most ferocious beasts can be rounded up, caught, caged, tamed, utilized or exploited. Or they can be exterminated and made to disappear from the face of the earth, as has already happened to some and will happen to others if humans do not improve in their behaviour. But there is one thing that the most powerful of men or the most extreme system cannot do: *enslave a cat*.'

CHARLES DUFF: *Ordinary Cats*

These are pieces of readable prose. Psychology and politics are subjects in which many writers are liable to use the most wearisome polysyllabic jargon or the most meaningless clichés; the books quoted above are relatively refreshingly free from such defects of style. The inferior type of thriller is often written in extremely bad English, ungrammatical, cliché-ridden and full of unnecessary exclamation marks; but here we see the decent style of a competent detective story. Animal books are often nauseatingly sentimental; here is one that is written by a man with some feeling for English. These authors say what they mean in correct English and do not irritate or bewilder the reader. They are free from such faults as over-long or ill-constructed sentences, accidental jingles, excessive alliteration or clumsy monotony of rhythm. They can all be read aloud easily and smoothly by any competent reader. Yet there is nothing in these passages that strikes us as memorably individual, no distinguishing uniqueness of style.

This sensible, workmanlike English that any educated adult ought to be able to learn to write with a little practice and some willingness to take trouble may be called the common style. Individual style is found mostly, with some interesting exceptions, in writers whose primary interests are literary.

The difference between individual and common style is the difference between art and craftsmanship.

Almost any intelligent person, with a suitable environment, adequate physique and proper training, can learn a craft; indeed, if this were not so most of us would live in a state of helpless misery. Everyone in the course of a normal life has to master a large number of skills, and human adaptability is astonishing. Very few people are able to paint in such a way as to be worthy of comparison with Leonardo da Vinci, compose music at the level of Bach or write as well as Shakespeare. This kind of achievement requires not only all the diligence and training, this time a never-ending training, that goes to perfection in any craft, but a very strong natural bent and, probably, a fanatical urge to pursue the art. Great art is a vocation. Art, as opposed to craft, is not necessarily found only among the 'fine arts'. Recently, in Switzerland, I saw a few carvings, notably an unforgettable eagle and owl, which were more than craftsmanship, much more than photographs in wood; among trivial and ordinary souvenirs they had a passion animating them. The distinction is difficult to make but can usually be felt. Similarly there is a good common prose style that may be learned, and a more intense, individual, exciting prose that is art, the expression of a powerful personality.

Probably for some purposes the common style is actually better than individual style, or at least a violently individual style. Textbooks and other purely informative books, practical instructions, reports, business letters, the more cool and rational types of argumentative prose, newspaper articles and light novels are generally written in common style and are none the worse for it. Great fiction, the works of outstanding essayists and historians, the reviews in the best weeklies, great argumentative prose of the kind which includes a strong appeal to emotion, short stories of the experimental type, unusual travel books and most good humorous prose are usually written in a noticeably individual style. Here are some examples of individual style; the reader may like to try to identify the authors before the names are given at the end.

1. 'Truth indeed came once into the world with her divine Master, and was a perfect shape most glorious to look on; but when he ascended, and his apostles after him were laid asleep, then straight arose a wicked race of deceivers, who, as that story goes of the Egyptian Typhon with his conspirators, how they dealt with the good Osiris, took the virgin Truth, hewed her lovely form into a thousand pieces, and scattered them to the four winds. From this time ever since, the sad friends of Truth, such as durst appear, imitating the careful search that

Isis made for the mangled body of Osiris, went up and down gathering up limb by limb still as they should find them. We have not yet found them all, Lords and Commons, nor ever shall do, till her Master's second coming; he shall bring together every joint and member, and shall mould them into an immortal feature of loveliness and perfection.'

2. 'And so Marat People's-friend is ended; the lone Stylites has got hurled down suddenly from his Pillar—*whitherward*. He that made him knows. Patriot Paris may sound triple and ten-fold, in dole and wail; re-echoed by Patriot France; and the Convention, 'Chabot, pale with terror, declaring that they are to be all assassinated', may decree him Pantheon Honours, Public Funeral, Mirabeau's dust making way for him; and Jacobin Societies, in lamentable oratory, summing up his character, parallel him to One, whom they think it honour to call 'the good Sansculotte',—whom we name not here; also a Chapel may be made, for the urn that holds his Heart, in the Place du Carrousel; and new-born children be named Marat; and Lago-di-Como Hawkers bake mountains of stucco into unbeautiful Busts; and David paint his Picture, or Death-Scene; and such other Apotheosis take place as the human genius, in these circumstances, can devise: but Marat returns no more to the light of this Sun.'

3. 'No, she said, she did not want a pear. Indeed, she had been keeping guard over the dish of fruit (without realising it) jealously, hoping that nobody would touch it. Her eyes had been going in and out among the curves and shadows of the fruit, among the rich purples of the lowland grapes, then over the horny ridge of the shell, putting a yellow against a purple, a curved shape against a round shape, without knowing why she did it, or why, every time she did it, she felt more and more serene; until, oh, what a pity that they should do it—a hand reached out, took a pear and spoilt the whole thing.

4. But if (fie of such a but) you be borne so neere the dull

making *Cataphract* of *Nilus* that you cannot heare the Plannet-like Musick of Poetrie, if you have so earth-creeping a mind that it cannot lift it selfe up to looke to the sky of Poetry, or rather, by a certaine rusticall disdaine, will become such a Mome as to be a *Momus* of Poetry; then, though I will not wish unto you the Asses ears of *Midas*, not to be driven by a Poets verses (as *Bubonax* was) to hang himselfe, nor to be rimed to death, as is said to be done in Ireland; yet this much curse I must send you, in the behalfe of all Poets, that while you live, you live in love, and never get favour for lacking skill of a *Sonnet*; and when you die, your memory die from the earth for want of an *Epitaph*.'

The reader will surely have felt without hesitation that these passages are more distinctive in style than the examples of common style quoted previously. The sources are as follows:

1. Milton: *Areopagitica*.
2. Carlyle: *The French Revolution*.
3. Virginia Woolf: *To the Lighthouse*.
4. Sir Philip Sidney: *Apologie for Poetrie*.

Style is a difficult thing to define in any way, and individual style is harder to define than common style; Lord Berners and James Joyce, Sir Thomas Browne and Addison, D. H. Lawrence and Mark Twain, have individual styles and a generalization which will cover all these will be too loose to be of much value. However, the reader will probably notice, in examining authors who are agreed upon as having an individual style, that such authors generally have a sensitive ear for rhythm, a characteristic choice of vocabulary, an inventiveness of phrase not found in more commonplace writers, a carefulness in the choice of words that may often amount to an almost scientific precision on subjects concerning which ordinary writers are apt to be vague and a greater power of varying rhythm and sentence structure to suit the mood of the moment. If a style can be parodied, it is either individual or so near illiteracy that its badness distinguishes it; if it cannot be parodied by any effort it is probably common style.

What causes this important difference in prose styles? For this is the essential difference, the first classification to be made when we are examining a piece of prose. It is probably true to say that individual style springs from a strong personality; certainly most artists of merit have strong personalities;[1] but it is not conversely true to say that all who write common style have little personality; I have known several writers of common style who had very vivid personalities. Genius always eludes definition.

It may, however, be worth while to suggest that two partial reasons for individuality of style are individuality of personality and uniqueness of subject matter—a psychological and a functional cause. It is impossible to write an individual style without being an individual, though having a lively personality does not enable a man to express it on paper. Perhaps it might be safe to say that the literary genius which produces (among other things) individual style in prose is made up of strong personality plus conscious craftsmanship plus a natural bent for language.

It may also be at least suspected that originality of thought will lead to originality of style. The person who has original thoughts is likely to be more intelligent than the person who does not, and thus will also be skilled in the handling of words —though there are exceptions. More important is the fact that the writer who has something new to say will discover that no style as yet available will serve and that a new style

[1] This is not to be confused with so-called 'artistic temperament'; artists are more sensitive than most people, but foolish tantrums are not a mark of the great artist.

must be devised to express these particular thoughts. Laura Riding and E. E. Cummings in poetry, Virginia Woolf, William Faulkner, and James Joyce in prose are notable recent examples of this. This is one reason why ill-educated people find it almost impossible to read the experimental work that is often one of the chief delights of the educated; original matter combined with a puzzling use of words asks too much of them.

However, this connection is not invariable. Lenin was a very important original thinker, but his style, in what I presume is a careful translation, seems to be unattractive and often clumsy. Bertrand Russell has originality of thought, but the common style, well handled, serves his purposes adequately; so far as I know Jane Austen has nothing original to say, but her style is unmistakable and a perpetual delight.

Another point that must be borne in mind when we consider individual styles is that a writer may develop in the course of a literary career. The style of Virginia Woolf in *Night and Day* is quite different from that of the later book *The Waves*; and such books as *The Common Reader* and *A Room of One's Own* differ in important features from the novels because their function is different. Fielding's *Joseph Andrews* and *Amelia* have considerable differences of style, and Fanny Burney's change—this time a degeneration—from *Evelina* to *Camilla* is one of the commonplaces of literary history. It is often difficult to trace a writer's development from stylistic fumbling to the creating of a truly individual style, because often the fumbling works are never printed; but it can probably be assumed that they once existed.

VIII. COMMON STYLE AND CHEAP STYLE

English is the language of the illiterate Vulgar. . . .

JOHN LOCKE: *Some Thoughts concerning Education*

THE common style is a good style; there is also what might, perhaps, be called the cheap style. It is cheap because it costs nothing—no effort goes to its making and it is cheap and nasty. Unfortunately, the inexperienced reader can sometimes be deceived by shoddiness and value a spurious, slovenly pseudo-ornamentation more than a vigorous simplicity. This is not a fault much to be blamed in the inexperienced; small children love long words for their impressive sound and the love of decoration has led to much human art; taste develops later than creativeness.

I have a friend who is a Civil Servant. Before she was married she had a flat in Chelsea and a charwoman used to come in the mornings to clean it. One day, to my friend's delight, she left the following note (I have, of course, changed the two names):

'Dear Miss Dixon,
    When I was cleening this morning 2 large mouses jump out of box will ask Man what to get for them.
                                    yours respectfully
                                            MRS. PETERS.'

Now, Mrs. Peters was semi-literate and ignorant. A woman with a better education would have known that *cleaning* is spelt with an *ea*; that it is not usual to write small numbers in figures in a formal letter; that the plural of *mouse* is *mice*; that English past tenses usually end in *ed*; that the indefinite or definite article is required in front of *box* in such a sentence; that sentences cannot be run together with a sudden change of subject implied; that common nouns in English are not capitalized; that *yours respectfully* and the mode of signature are vulgarisms. Mrs. Peters needed to learn a great deal about letter-writing; yet when we consider her poor verbal powers and limited education her effort to convey important information politely is worthy of respect. No words are wasted and the meaning is clear. Miss Dixon is the best kind of Civil Servant; but the wrong kind might have translated Mrs. Peters's effort into this kind of language:

'*Rodent Extermination Department,*
Whitehall.

'*Your Ref.:* MUS/DOM/2/OUT.
To Miss Dixon:
Dear Madam,

In the course of proceedings whose overall target was the hygienic rehabilitation of your dwelling quarters, the attention of the appropriate operative was drawn to the localized activities of two rodents in a state of obvious nutritional adequacy and physical activity. Consultations with a higher authority with a view to placing ourselves in a position to adopt the appropriate methods for the liquidation of this surplus population will begin at the earliest available opportunity.

I beg to remain, Madam,
Your obedient servant,
M. PETERS.'

Poor Mrs. Peters would be impressed by this, no doubt; but it is a far worse letter than her own. If we remove the faults due to mere ignorance from her letter we have a sensible, concise and polite message:

'Dear Miss Dixon,

While I was cleaning, this morning, two large mice jumped out of a box; I will ask a man I know what to buy to kill them.

Yours sincerely,
M. PETERS.'

The 'Civil Service' letter takes three times as long to say the same thing in ugly, clumsy language of a kind that is alarming and puzzling to uneducated people.

This example is not fair to the Civil Service; it is probably only a minority of Civil Servants nowadays who write this kind of ugly jargon;[1] but it is still too popular. This type of cheap English is also to be found in the letters of some business firms. It is a pity that nowadays people who read little are more likely to model any prose they have to write on the newspaper or even the 'comic' than on the old model, the Bible and perhaps Bunyan.[2]

It may be thought that 'Civil Service' jargon, since it is certainly not individual, is the common style; it is not; the common style is simple, forceful at its best, and always direct. 'Civil Service' style is characterized by heavy circumlocutions, a love of long words and a set of hackneyed phrases that either mean nothing ('in a position to', 'with regard to', 'taking everything into consideration') or are long-winded ways of saying something that could be said much better in a few syllables ('appropriate remuneration for personnel en-

[1] Especially since the two admirable attacks by Sir Ernest Gowers in *Plain Words* and *An A.B.C. of Plain Words*.

[2] Many adults of low intelligence read children's 'comics' and there are even 'comics' for adults—a disturbing thought.

gaged in rodent extermination' = the right pay for those who catch rats and mice).

Another kind of cheap and nasty style is to be found in many advertisements. Here are a few monstrosities:

'You'll be nearer and dearer to the lady of your life when you give your face the treat of ——.'

(Notice the horrible coyness of this, the incapacity to call a sweetheart a sweetheart.)

'For a smooth, full-flavoured man's smoke —— is miles ahead. Men in all walks of life find this fresh, rich tobacco gives a deep satisfaction that remains long after each pipeful. Try it today—discover the richest joy in smoking.'

(A slovenliness in the choice of words that is worse than mere ignorance of vocabulary; the whole flavour of the copy is to give to smoking the kind of language that should be kept for important satisfactions.)

'Now men can be bright in the morning! *Now*—even on a cold day—shaving won't be so bad.'

(This is a fragment of a particularly nerve-grating advertisement. The same shaving preparation is 'gloriously soothing' and the copywriter refers in one paragraph to wives as 'the ladies', 'the womenfolk' and 'the darlings'—surely an accumulation of coyness and superiority to make any decent husband squirm! The fragment quoted above not only has vulgar italicizing—usually a confession that the writer cannot arrange his words so as to make the emphasis fall on the important word naturally—but suggests a singular want of manliness in men.)

We all know the meaninglessness of such words as 'outstanding', 'perfected', 'super-efficient', 'revolutionary', 'miraculous', 'invaluable', in advertisements; good, useful and once evocative words lose all their force by such dilutions, so much so that I once found in a catalogue 'This novelty is new'!

Common Style and Cheap Style

Advertising copy is probably the worst English to be found today in print. It is full of exaggerations, the misuse of words, vulgarisms, ugly coinages—many trade names are themselves an offence against aesthetics—childish jokes, cheap ways of giving emphasis, pseudo-scientific language and other atrocities. The reader will easily find dozens of examples in any magazine, though it must be admitted that some modern advertising is quite good in style and even witty or dignified.[1] Unfortunately many people are not naturally sensitive to diction and are not moved to protest against such abuses of language as are found every day in the Press. There are a number of otherwise satisfactory goods that ought to be boycotted by all lovers of good English until their copywriters grow up and write for people who have grown up.

Humorous writing can be a fine art; the essays of Robert Lynd, Charles Lamb, Rose Macaulay and G. K. Chesterton should be sufficient evidence of that; but in this country standards of humour are low and many humorous articles depend for their effect on cheap devices such as mis-spelling—unfortunately a favourite brand of false humour in the children's comic, where it is obviously undesirable because it confuses children who are just learning to spell—facetious phrases, childish euphemisms and bad puns. Most of the humour to be found in school magazines shows very clearly how our first attempts at humour are cheaply facetious and lack subtlety or originality; but the humour of the average school magazine, having been vetted by a teacher, is much better than that of the average adult 'comic paper'.[2]

The bad novel is another ever-flowing spring of cheap-and-

[1] The advertisements quoted have been altered in some particular to avoid giving offence; for it would be unkind to single out a few offenders when every daily paper is full of offences.

[2] *Punch*, *Lilliput* and *London Opinion* are among those humour magazines in which most contributors have a sense of style.

nasty style; for the writer who turns out tripe by the yard has no time to make the necessary effort to write the common style. In the bad thriller[2] there are usually far too many exclamation marks; all the characters speak alike; words are used inaccurately by a writer who obviously never looks in the dictionary when he is in doubt about a word, because he has not enough feeling for words to be in doubt about any of them. I have met astonishing malapropisms in such books: people who think *deprecate* and *depreciate* mean the same, or that *half-caste* is to do with social position, and people who use the word *native* to mean a negro in Kent, can apparently achieve publication. In such novels, too, everyone falls with a *sickening thud* and everything remarkable happens at the *psychological moment*. Bad love stories are often even worse, with a lushness of style that is all the more revolting by its attempt at sublimity.

One of the causes of various kinds of grossly bad style such as may be called cheap instead of common is that we all tend to feel that the decorated is of more value than the plain. This in itself leads to many refinements, amenities and beauties; but it also leads people who, with training, might write the common style admirably, to try to write something more adorned and thus to fall into one of the many traps of what Osbert Lancaster, in a coinage I wish I had made myself, calls, in architecture, 'Pseudish'. Some discussion of the virtues and proper functions of simplicity and ornamentation may therefore be helpful.

[2] Though some school teachers refuse to admit it, not all thrillers are badly written: Conan Doyle, John Buchan, Michael Innes, Eric Ambler have even individual style—and Graham Greene has written thrillers.

IX. SIMPLICITY AND ORNAMENTATION

The style of an author should be the image of his mind, but the choice and command of language is the fruit of exercise. Many experiments were made before I could hit the middle line between a dull chronicle and a rhetorical declamation: three times did I compose the first chapter, and twice the second and third, before I was tolerably satisfied with their effect.

EDWARD GIBBON: *Autobiography*

THE common style is reasonably simple, for in the use of ornaments we soon show our individual tendencies; outside parody and the weakly imitative no two people are likely to hit upon precisely the same method of achieving special effects by special means. An individual style may, however, range from extreme simplicity and directness to the most elaborately decorated style.

Here two fallacies may be exploded. One, commonest among people of little education or immature taste, is the belief that nothing is beautiful that is not ornamented and that ornament is something to be put on to a work of art afterwards, like fondants on an iced cake. This is a misconception which one look at the full moon, the sea or the face of a pretty child ought to disprove. A good ornamental style is an organic whole; the ornamentation is not an afterthought conscientiously applied, but is dictated by the whole tone of the piece and temperament of the writer, like rhythm in poetry.

Simplicity and Ornamentation

Educated people with some maturity of taste, however, are at present liable to be trapped by another fallacy which is at present fashionable, the idea that any ornamental style is in some way 'phoney' or 'pseudo'; they are so wedded to the beauty of simplicity that in their healthy preference for a plain spherical lamp rather than an unfunctional coloured shade with irrelevant curves and painted ships all round it they believe that there are no beautiful chandeliers. Certainly there are not many, and a chandelier would be quite out of place in a modern study-bedroom; but there are some that are admirable in a large hall with a high ceiling. Jewellery and cosmetics that would look vulgarly ostentatious in the greengrocer's might look smart and dignified at a formal ball. In general what is real individual style, however elaborate and formal, is beautiful and exciting, for the form springs from within; feeble imitations and pompous clichés are what give a style an air of insincerity and shoddiness.

Questions of taste can never be finally settled. If people are unaffected by something which seems beautiful to other people, that does not much matter, provided that both sides can discuss the matter honestly and politely. Perhaps a rough generalization in the matter of ornament may be made thus: the function of the style should be the criterion of its fitness. Rich rhetorical decoration would be grossly and grotesquely out of place in a cookery book:

APPLE PIE

'Of those fruits that are the innocent equivalents, the unsymbolic relicts, of the deadly growth of the primal Eden, take such a sufficiency as may fill a piedish when they are flayed and disembowelled, that is, stripped of their peel, the outer husk and coloured garment, and of the inner implications of futurity, the pips. Let these white segments be laid in the dish with two or three Indian cloves, seasoned with a shower of sugar and perhaps with a touch of Lamb's 'fragrant cinnamon'. Now you shall prepare a pastry, and make a kind of lid or roof over the dismembered apples and exposed limbs of the fruit. This lid must be trimmed to the shape of the piedish, and in the centre thereof let there be a hole, that the steam from the martyred fruit may arise like fumes from Vesuvius, for otherwise your paste may perchance become sodden and misshapen. It is good to provide a funnel such as is made for this purpose, or, failing that, some succedaneum and prop such as an egg-cup may be set beneath the prudent aperture. The lid may be adorned as your fancy dictates, with leaves of pastry, a pastry crown, rims and curls in diverse patterns; but afterwards you must bake your pie in a fairly hot oven till it be brown and ready.'

Not only is this style out of place in the context, but its wordiness makes it necessary for me to leave out such details as how to make the pastry, and the proper heat of the oven, which would be more useful to an inexperienced cook than these inappropriate figures of speech.

It is easy to laugh at misapplied ornament, but there are occasions when simplicity would sound absurd and childish. A Royal Proclamation, a speech in praise of a dead hero or on some great occasion, a solemn religious service of the formal kind, a letter to someone loved and honoured, do genuinely demand a certain colour and richness of style. Sir Thomas Bodley's famous letter to the Vice-Chancellor of Oxford, with figures of speech, alliterations, long sentences and massive rhythms, is very suitable to the solemn project for founding a great library; anyone who has ever stood in the sombre and noble quadrangle of the Old Bodleian will not feel that the style is too dignified for the matter:

'Sir, although you know me not, as I suppose, yet for the furthering of an offer, of evident utility, to your whole University, I will not be too scrupulous in craving your assistance. I have always been of a mind that if God, of his goodness, should make me able to do anything for the benefit of posterity, I would show some token of affection that I have ever borne to the studies of good Learning. I know my portion is too slender to perform, for the present, any answerable act to my willing disposition: but yet, to notify some part of my desire in that behalf, I have resolved thus to deal. Where there hath been heretofore a public library in Oxford, which, you know, is apparent by the room itself remaining, and by your statute Records, I will take the charge and cost upon me, to reduce it again to his former use: and to make it fit, and handsome with seats, and shelves, and desks, and all that may be needful to stir up other men's benevolence to help to furnish it with books. And this I purpose to begin, as soon as timber can be gotten, to the intent that you may reap some speedy Profit of my Project. And where before, as I conceive, it was to be reputed but a store of books of diverse benefactors, because it never had any lasting allowance, for augmentation of the Number, or supply of Books decayed: whereby it came to pass that when those that were in it were either wasted or embezzled, the whole Foundation came to ruin: to meet with that inconvenience, I will so provide hereafter (if God do not hinder my present design) as you shall be still assured of a standing annual rent, to be disbursed every year in buying of books, in officers' stipends, and other pertinent occasions, with which provision, and some order for preservation of the place, and of the furniture of it, from accustomed abuses, it may perhaps in time to come prove a notable Treasure for the multitude of volumes, an excellent benefit for the use and case of students, and a singular ornament in the University. . . . Which is now as much as I can think on, whereunto, at your good leisure, I would request your friendly answer. And if it lie in my ability to deserve your pains in that behalf, although

we be not yet acquainted, you shall find me very forward.
From London, Feb. 23, 1597.

Your Affectionate Friend,
THO: BODLEY.'

The reader should, however, be careful not to confuse archaism with ornamentation. Almost anything written before 1800 will look stylistically unusual to anyone not already familiar with the historical study of literature. False archaism —the imitation of old styles or the borrowing of obsolete words—is sometimes called *Wardour Street English*; I have committed some of this in my apple-pie recipe. Much in the Bible, Shakespeare, or Bunyan that to our ears sounds unusual and decorative was probably simply the language of the times; and because a word has lost its familiarity we cannot assume, without consulting a large dictionary, that it was rare at all times. It is impossible to say that a style was 'common' in its own day, or 'individual', until we have read a great deal of the writing of the period in question.

Real simplicity is not at all easy to achieve; the greatest simple styles have a directness that few of us can hope to imitate. If simplicity were natural to us we should not so often feel compelled to use such expressions as : 'I wish I could tell you how I feel!' or 'Let me try to make this clear'. It was a great artist in words, De Quincey, who spoke of 'the agony of the incommunicable'. Here are some fine examples of simple style; it will be observed that, though simple, they are also individual.

'I lay down on the grass, which was very short and soft, where I slept sounder than ever I remembered to have done in my life, and, as I reckoned, above nine hours, for when I awaked it was just daylight. I attempted to rise, but was not able to stir; for as I happened to lie on my back, I found my arms and legs were strongly fastened on each side to the ground, and my hair, which was long and thick, tied down in the same manner. I likewise felt several slender ligatures across my body, from my arm-pits to my thighs. I could only look upwards; the sun began to grow hot, and the light offended mine eyes. I heard a confused noise about me, but, in the posture I lay, could see nothing except the sky. In a little time I felt something alive moving on my left leg which, advancing gently forward over my breast, came up almost to my chin, when, bending mine eyes downwards as much as I could, I perceived it to be a human creature not six inches high, with a bow and arrow in his hands, and a quiver at his back.'

JONATHAN SWIFT: *Gulliver's Travels*

'Well, then, he said, he would have me promise to go and fetch him all the money I had, every farthing. I told him I would, and I went into my chamber and fetched him a little private drawer, where I had about six guineas more, and some silver, and threw it all down upon the bed, and bade me open a little walnut-tree box he had upon the table, and bring him such a drawer, which I did. In which drawer there was a great deal of money in gold, I believe near two hundred guineas, but I knew not how much. He took the drawer, and taking my hand, made me put it in and take a whole handful. I was backward at that, but he held my hand hard in his hand, and put it into the drawer, and made me take out as many guineas almost as I could well take up at once.'

DANIEL DEFOE: *Moll Flanders*

'In Allahabad my mother was in a procession which was stopped by the police and later charged with *lathis*. When the procession had been halted someone brought her a chair, and she was sitting on this on the road at the head of the procession. Some people who were especially looking after her, including my secretary, were arrested and removed, and then came the police charge. My mother was knocked down from her chair, and was hit repeatedly on the head with canes. Blood came out of an open wound in the head; she fainted, and lay on the roadside, which had now been cleared of processionists and public. After some time she was picked up and brought by a police officer in his car to Anand Bhawan. That night a false rumour spread in Allahabad that my mother had died. Angry crowds gathered together, forgot about peace and non-violence, and attacked the police. There was firing by the police, resulting in the death of some people.

'When the news of all this came to me some days after the occurrence (for we had a weekly paper), the thought of my frail old mother lying bleeding on the dusty road obsessed me, and I wondered how I would have behaved if I had been there.'

JAWAHARLAL NEHRU: *Autobiography*[1]

'Don Manuel sent for the tailor. He could be very affable when he chose, and when his measurements had been taken and various materials examined he set himself to be so. As natives of the same city they had certain common interests and Don Manuel talked to him good-humouredly of the changes that had taken place in it during his long absence. The tailor was a little dried-up man with a sharp nose and a querulous expression. But he was garrulous. Finding in Don Manuel a sympathetic listener he enlarged upon the hard times. The wars and the heavy taxation had impoverished everyone, and even gentlemen of the highest rank were content to wear their clothes till they were threadbare. It was not so easy to make a good living then as it had been thirty years before when the caravels were arriving regularly with their cargo of gold from

[1] English people who will not trouble to write their own language well ought to be shamed by reading the English of such Indian writers as Pandit Jawaharlal Nehru, his sister Krishna Nehru, Rabindranath Tagore, Mulk Raj Anand, D. F. Karaka, Professor Radhakrishnan and a number of obscure Indians to be met in British universities.

America. A few well-directed questions brought out the fact that he was worried about his son. . . . It was only right that he should follow in his father's footsteps, but the boy had silly ideas and it had required the exercise of parental authority to force him to go into the business.'

SOMERSET MAUGHAM: *Catalina*

These are fine examples of direct, simple English without obvious adornment. Even with such good English the pedant might find fault; Swift's rhyme eyes/sky would have been better avoided; Mr. Maugham's pronouns are twice technically ambiguous, though as common sense tells us at once which person is meant it would be mere fuss and carping to complain. In each of these passages we are able to picture a situation without effort and also to attach to it the right kind of emotion. In all the pieces, and still more in a larger sample of the book, we notice how simplicity need not lose individuality.

Swift's style is, here, probably the most formal. He has the longest sentences, but handles them so that they are not in the least cumbersome.[1] Defoe achieves verisimilitude partly by his constant slight flavour of the colloquial; we seem to hear his principal characters engaged in reminiscence. Pandit Nehru appears to make his impression by simple statement, though actually his impressively sincere and natural style is probably the fruit of a very fine conscious or unconscious selection. The introduction of a personal emotion here is the more effective and convincing for the absolute quiet—and the careful doing of justice to the decent enemy—of the actual statement preceding it. Mr. Maugham's style, always a fine example of the simple style, nearly always carries as its personal flavour a hint of irony, often of ironic compassion; even in this passage irony is not far away.

[1] Swift was something of a fanatic for pure English and commented on many current abuses of language.

Ornament in style may be of many kinds. It is usually easier to talk critically about an ornamental style, because the topics of comment are more obvious. A piece of prose may be enriched by many figures of speech which are classified in various ancient and modern books on rhetoric. A concise style is not necessarily without ornament; there is a kind of very epigrammatical style in which the conciseness itself is not only the individuality of the style but its decoration. Some of the essays of Francis Bacon are the obvious example of this; here is an example that is rather less widely known:

'A discontented man is one that is fallen out with the world, and will be revenged on himself. Fortune has denied him in something, and he now takes pet, and will be miserable in spite. The root of his disease is a self-humouring pride, and an accustomed tenderness, not to be crossed in his fancy; and the occasions commonly one of these three, a hard father, a peevish wench, or his ambition thwarted. He considered not the nature of the world till he felt it, and all blows fall on him heavier, because they light not first on his expectation. He has now forgone all but his pride, and is yet vainglorious in the ostentation of his melancholy.'

JOHN EARLE: *Micro-Cosmographie*

The greatest period for very ornate style was probably the Elizabethan and Jacobean period; but there have been writers of ornate style at all periods. Some of them include Francis Bacon, Lord Berners, the translator of Froissart, John Florio (the translator of Montaigne), Shakespeare in much of his dramatic prose, such as the long speeches of Falstaff; such Euphuistic writers as John Lyly, Thomas Lodge and Sir Philip Sidney; John Donne, Sir Thomas Browne, Robert Burton, Izaak Walton in the period mentioned above; later there are Edmund Burke, Thomas Carlyle, John Ruskin, Thomas De Quincey, Charles Lamb, William Hazlitt, Charles

93

Dickens, Edward Gibbon, Henry Fielding (in the ironical mock-heroic vein that was his first prose style in fiction), Samuel Johnson, and Lord Macaulay; in the present age writers of an ornate style have included Joseph Conrad, G. K. Chesterton, Virginia Woolf, James Joyce, D. H. Lawrence, and a number of good minor writers who are often counted as freaks, such as Mervyn Peake and Dylan Thomas.[1] Today, however, the simple style is usually preferred for ordinary light literature and for the newspapers, which are, all too exclusively, the models for style studied unconsciously, by people who read little else.

An elaborate classification of the ornaments of style will be given later in the chapter on Rhetoric. First, however, some other general classifications of prose style may be useful.

[1] Dylan Thomas, a 'minor' writer of prose, is an important poet.

X. SUBDIVISIONS

(A) OBJECTIVE AND SUBJECTIVE

> This was the time, when, all things tending fast
> To depravation, speculative schemes—
> That promised to abstract the hopes of Man
> Out of his feelings, to be fixed thenceforth
> For ever in a purer element—
> Found ready welcome.
>
> WORDSWORTH: *The Prelude, Book XI*

WHEN we examine a style we are helped by a realization of how far it is objective or subjective, and it is often necessary to think hard about this. *Objective* in the sense, 'looking at what is seen and not letting personal feelings come into the picture' and *subjective* in the sense, 'from the point of view of the observer, coloured by personal feelings' are critical terms that have developed much later than the terms of rhetoric and comparatively late in literary history altogether; they seem to have appeared first in these senses round about the beginning of the eighteenth century, but are not common in eighteenth-century criticism.

A book describing scientific experiments is, or should be, almost completely objective. It we wish to imagine pure objectivity we may think of a proof in geometry. An autobiography is expected to be fairly subjective. Most argumentative prose and fiction will stand somewhere between these two.

Subdivisions, A. Objective and Subjective

A difficulty in making this subdivision is that there are two kinds of subjectivity and objectivity in literary criticism; one is stylistic and easy to define; the other might be called moral or psychological. Four examples made up for the purpose may illustrate this:

1. *Objective* (*style*)

'Outside my window there is a grey path, a green lawn and a patch of brown earth in which a number of bushes of different sizes are planted. The bushes are evergreens; the trees behind them have lost their leaves and are therefore bare. There are some more bare trees and a few green bushes, mostly laurels, on the other side of the lawn. A thrush is looking for worms on the lawn.'

There is nothing here but a description of what I can see; my eye is on the object. My own feelings are excluded and no adjective or phrase hints in any way at my feelings indirectly. It is possible to treat the same view more subjectively.

2. *Subjective* (*style*)

'I can see, through my window, a grey path that reminds me of the grey road outside in this dismal weather. The lawn is green, the colour of hope; the trees are bare, stripped like me of most of the hopes of spring. A hungry thrush is looking for worms on the lawn. At present the only comfort for sad eyes is to be found in the evergreen bushes, which prove that winter itself does not defeat all growth, and in the laurels among the evergreens, reminding me that literature may be more lasting than human sufferings.'

This description of the same scene is quite different in tone; I am thinking about my own feelings and the scene is merely an excuse for a frank expression of personal conflicts. The subject is important—the one who is looking at the scene.

This is easy. We may, however, have an objective style in

which subjective feelings have played a great part, or a style that appears to be subjective when actually the writer is being objective about himself, a detached observer. This kind of paradox of style is much more difficult to discuss.

3. Subjective (*psychological*)

'The view is grey, drab and depressing. Nothing can be seen but a lawn, a path, a few trees and bushes; the only live thing visible is a thrush. The sky overhead is a slaty grey and the sun is not shining. The path is visibly damp. The leafless trees are grey and motionless.'

This sounds like objectivity; there is nothing but a description of the view, with no comment on personal feelings or any 'I'. Yet if this description is compared with No. 1 the reader will notice how in 3 I have really allowed the description to be affected by my personal feelings of depression, wording the account of the scene in such a way as to stress its drabness. The description 1 is really more accurate.

4. Objective (*psychological*)

'It seems that today I am suffering from a fit of depression. Perhaps this is because I have a slight cold and this is making me feel vaguely unwell. I seem to unable to take pleasure in what is really quite an agreeable view of a lawn, trees, bushes and a path. Perhaps I shall see it in a different light when my health is better.'

This is all about 'I', but, as is often found in good auto-biographies, especially modern ones,[1] the writer is treating the 'I' objectively; I do not assume that my feelings are correct and am trying to look at them as a doctor or psychologist would, in order to understand them. Thus, though the style suggests, at first sight, subjectivity, the psychological atmosphere is one of objectivity.

[1] A recent example is Stephen Spender's *World within World*.

Thus it is dangerous to assume that everything that omits all mention of personal feelings is entirely objective or that anything full of 'I' is wholly subjective. Indeed, I often find it necessary to explain to students, who have been brought up to avoid the 'I' in written work as 'egotistical', that often 'I think the moon is made of green cheese' is much more modest and really much more objective, that 'Everyone knows that the moon is made of green cheese'. It is possible for an intelligent person to state his or her feelings about something with surprising objectivity at times—an honest recognition of personal limitations and possible causes for the feelings, but when we start generalizing recklessly we are more likely to be subjective without even realizing it.

A very common and useful literary device is to use the most objective style possible in order to carry out a purpose of psychological subjectivity; that is, to use what looks like straightforward description in order to share strong feelings with the reader; the air of sincerity and refusal to express an opinion adds to the force of the emotional attack. Any personal comment on this would weaken it:

'All the powder of the *Revenge* to the last barrel was now spent, all her pikes broken, forty of her best men slain, and the most part of the rest hurt. In the beginning of the fight she had but one hundred free from sickness, and fourscore and ten sick, laid in hold upon the ballast. A small troop to man such a ship, and a weak garrison to resist so mighty an army. By those hundred all was sustained, the volleys, boardings, and enterings of fifteen ships of war, besides those which beat her at large. On the contrary, the Spanish were always supplied with soldiers brought from every squadron: all manner of arms and powder at will. Unto ours there remained no comfort at all, no hope, no supply either of ships, men, or weapons; the masts all beaten overboard, all her tackle cut asunder, her upper work altogether rased, and in effect evened she was with the water, but the very foundation or bottom of a ship, nothing being left overhead either for flight or defence. Sir *Richard* finding himself in this distress, and unable any longer to make resistance, having endured in this fifteen hours' fight the assault of fifteen several Armadoes, all by turns aboard him, and by estimation eight hundred shot of great artillery, besides many assaults and entries; and that himself and the ship must needs be possessed by the enemy, who were now all cast in a ring about him; the *Revenge* not able to move one way or another, but as she was moved with the waves and billows of the sea: commanded the master Gunner, whom he knew to be a most resolute man, to split and sink the ship; that thereby nothing might remain of glory or victory to the Spaniards, seeing in so many hours' fight, and with so great a Navy they were not able to take her, having had fifteen hours' time, fifteen thousand men, and fifty and three sail of men-of-war to perform it withal: and perswaded the company, or as many as he could induce, to yield themselves unto God, and to the mercy of none else; but as they had like valiant resolute men repulsed so many enemies, they should not now shorten the honour of their nation, by prolonging their own lives for a few hours, or a few days.'

SIR WALTER RALEIGH: *A Report of the Truth of the Fight about the Isle of Azores*

The subjective is not, of course, always weak; the emotions of a strong personality, even when we feel that the speaker is wrong-headed, may be impressive. Nothing can be more objectionable to an educated person of today in England than the view of Nathaniel Ward (1578-1652) that religious toleration was a sin and an error; but certainly the intrusion of personal feeling does not weaken his argument here:

'It is said, though a man have light enough himself to see in the truth, yet if he hath not enough to enlighten others he is bound to tolerate them. I will engage myself that all the devils in Britanie shall sell themselves to their shirts to purchase a lease of this position for three of their lives, under the the seal of the Parliament.

It is said that men ought to have liberty of their conscience, and that it is persecution to debar them of it: I can rather stand amazed than reply to this: it is an astonishment to think that the brains of men should be parboiled in such impious ignorance. Let all the wits under the heavens lay their heads together and find an assertion worse than this (one excepted) I will petition to be chosen the universal idiot of the world.'

There is really nothing here but personal feeling; yet its vehemence is such that it sounds almost like real argument.

Much apparently objective argument, as in political pamphlets, religious tracts and statements about education, as well as much historical writing, is really prompted by, or coloured by, personal feelings so strong as to give some degree of subjectivity to the work. This is true to a lesser extent even in such fields as science or literary criticism. This present book is intended to be an objective study of prose style for the guidance of students; but I do not doubt that here and there my own emotions and experiences colour the matter somewhat; complete objectivity in anything except mathematics is probably an illusion.

It will be clear from this chapter that anyone who wishes to be a responsible literary critic must also be something of a psychologist. If we are to assess the degree of objectivity—not forgetting that objectivity is not in itself a virtue except in the sciences, but knowing that an accurate appraisal of a style will depend in part on the writer's intentions—we must be skilled in appreciating the use of words as it shows the workings of the mind. No one ever knows enough psychology, but the study of the subject is illuminating in all matters of literary history and criticism.

XI. SUBDIVISIONS

(B) ABSTRACT AND CONCRETE

He who would do good to another must do it in Minute Particulars:
General Good is the plea of the scoundrel, hypocrite and flatterer,
For Art and Science cannot exist but in minutely organized Particulars
And not in generalizing Demonstrations of the Rational Power.

WILLIAM BLAKE: *Jerusalem, Book III*

EVERYONE knows the difference between abstract and
concrete in a rough way; that *bread, spade, nose, house,
puddle, snail* are concrete words—or, to be more
exact, words describing concrete things; that *hope, kindness,
love, intelligence, logic, bewilderment* are words describing abstract ideas. This difference may have an important effect on
prose style. Here is a piece of description about as extremely
concrete as a description could be.

'This made him very popular, always speaking kindly to
the husband, brother or father, who was to boot very wel-
come to his house whenever he came. There he found beef
pudding and small beer in great plenty, a house not so neatly
kept as to shame him or his dirty shoes, the great hall strewed
with marrow bones, full of hawks' perches, hounds, spaniels,
and terriers, the upper sides of the hall hung with the fox-
skins of this and the last year's skinning, here and there a pole-
cat intermixed, guns and keepers' and hunters' poles in
abundance. The parlour was a large long room, as properly
furnished; on a great hearth paved with brick lay some

terriers and the choicest hounds and spaniels; seldom but two of the great chairs had litters of young cats in them, which were not to be disturbed, he having always three or four attending him at dinner, and a little white round stick of fourteen inches long lying by his trencher, that he might defend such meat as he had no mind to part with to them. The windows, which were very large, served for places to lay his arrows, crossbows, stonebows and other such like accoutrements; the corners of the room full of the best chose hunting and hawking poles; an oyster-table at the lower end, which was of constant use twice a day all the year round, for he never failed to eat oysters before dinner and supper through all seasons: the neighbouring town of Poole supplied him with them.'

THE EARL OF SHAFTESBURY (1621-1683): *Fragment of Autobiography* (Shaftesbury Papers)

Here, in contrast, is a very abstract piece of literary criticism:

'I observed before, that it is often difficult to separate the qualities of Style from the qualities of Thought; and it is found so in this instance, for, in order to write with Precision, though this be properly a quality of Style, one must possess a very considerable degree of distinctness and accuracy in his manner of thinking.[1]

'The words, which a man uses to express his ideas, may be faulty in three respects: they may either not express that idea which the author intends, but some other which only resembles, or is a-kin to it; or, they may express that idea, but not quite fully and completely; or, they may express it, together with something more than he intends. Precision stands opposed to all these three faults; but chiefly to the last. In an author's writing with Propriety, his being free from the

---

[1] Nowadays the mixture of 'one' and 'his' is bad grammar.

two former faults seems implied. The words which he uses are proper; that is, they express that idea which he intends, and they express it fully; but to be Precise signifies, that they express that idea, and no more. There is nothing in his words which introduces any foreign idea, any superfluous unreasonable accessory, so as to mix it confusedly with the principal object, and thereby to render our conception of that object loose and indistinct. This requires a writer to have, himself, a very clear apprehension of the object he means to represent to us; to have laid fast hold of it in his mind; and never to waver in any one view he takes of it: a perfection to which, indeed, few writers attain.'

HUGH BLAIR: *Lectures on Rhetoric and Belles Lettres*

There is probably no reader of this book who cannot follow the first passage more easily than the second, although the second is a fairly easy piece of abstract writing.

Abstract ideas arise from the faculty of generalization and are both a product and a theme for reason; but the human mind, after thousands of years of civilization, still does not take very kindly to abstract thought. Many people of poor intelligence or education, and most young children, can understand only what they can either perceive by means of the sense, or imagine themselves perceiving by means of the senses. William Blake probably carried his distrust of Reason too far; it seems to be difficult to perceive the limitations of reason without also wishing to attack it; Lawrence had the same difficulty; but the example of 'Civil Service language' already given, and much of the language used in making political statements, shows how a preference for the abstract word to the concrete word may be a method of disguising the truth and bemusing the public. When we use abstract language without wishing to deceive, we generally have to use some concrete examples in order to make our meaning clear.

It is interesting to notice how Blair, in his next paragraph, uses a concrete image to help the reader:

'The use and importance of Precision, may be deduced from the nature of the human mind. It never can view, clearly and distinctly, above one object at a time. If it must look at two or three together, especially objects among which there is resemblance or connection, it finds itself confused and embarrassed. It cannot clearly perceive in what they agree, and in what they differ. Thus, were any object, suppose some animal, to be presented to me, of whose structure I wanted to form a distinct notion, I would desire all its trappings to be taken off, I would require it to be brought before me by itself, and to stand alone, that there might be nothing to distract my attention. The same is the case with words.'

Such analogies are almost a necessity for the normal reader. We also translate the abstract and the general into the concrete and particular by examples. 'We ought to be kind.'—'What is *kind*?' 'Oh, it is giving up your seat to old ladies on the bus, helping blind people across the road, comforting people in trouble, opening doors for people who have a lot to carry, saying pleasant things about people. . . .' At this point the hearer has some notion of what kindness means.

Moreover, no language can ever be completely abstract, for, to an astonishing extent, all language is full of buried metaphors.[1] In the Blair passage the alert student may already have noticed that *a-kin*, *stands opposed*, *laid fast hold of* and *waver* are inconspicuous metaphors; even the vague visualization allowed by these is some help to the reader. Many of our abstract words are concrete metaphors if we trace them back

[1] I am myself able to speak of few languages; but everything I have heard or read about any languages suggests that this is a general truth. It even happens in Esperanto.

to their derivation. Here are some examples that may surprise the reader.

distraction originally meant	*pulling apart*	
emotion	*shaken up, upheaved*	
instinct	*pricked with a goad*	(impelled)
zest	*lemon peel*	
life	*body*	
bless	*sprinkle with blood*	
humour	*moisture*	

These are explanations that need further commentary to be accurate, but it is interesting to trace the full story of each word by means of a dictionary.

When we are commenting upon a style, it may be helpful to notice when the abstract changes to the concrete or vice versa, when a concrete word is suddenly brought in to give a vivid picture and sense of reality, when a concrete analogy is used to explain something abstract—some of the greatest examples of this are to be found in the parables of Jesus—and when an abstract term disguises something which, in concrete terms, would be less acceptable.

It should not be supposed that the concrete is always to be preferred to the abstract; as with simplicity and ornamentation, objectivity and subjectivity, suitability will be the test. There are some ideas in philosophy and psychology that cannot be expressed at all in concrete language. Any analogies that were used would be misleading rather than helpful. On the other hand, it is impossible to tell anyone how to put a washer on the tap in abstract language. But if the reader is aware of the difference and of this incapacity of the human mind to grasp much abstraction at once much will be accounted for in prose style. For this incapacity leads to metaphor as soon as we begin to think about anything beyond immediate bodily preoccupations, and metaphor leads to poetry, which is the apotheosis of language.

From this it will follow that there are really two quite different kinds of concrete language. One is straight description: 'There are apples and grapes in the dish. I shall peel an apple with a fruit-knife and throw the coil of green and red peel into the glowing fire.' The other has the very different function of being metaphorical: 'The love of a man for a woman is like the force that draws the tides after the moon. The love of a woman for a man is often more like the urge that brings the rivers running to lose themselves in the ocean.' The first kind of concrete language is a product of observation or of visualization;[1] the second kind is the product of imagination. We find examples of concrete observation or visualization in Defoe, Fielding, and Hemingway; we find examples of concrete imagination in the sermons of Donne, in Jungian psychology, in the philosophy of Plato.

Abstract language can have no parallel subdivision, for until something concrete comes into it it is not figurative. At the same time, abstract nouns and ideas are often more ambiguous, because their meanings—precisely because of the difficulty we all have in conceiving abstractions—are liable to be different for different people. People often have alarmingly different ideas of what is meant by such words as *freedom, decency, democracy, morality, Christianity, sanity, justice, decadence, sin, rights, duties, love* and *truth*. We may demand freedom and get something that we are told is freedom, but that to us is more like slavery; if we ask for bread, we may receive a stone, but no one will call the stone bread. Thus we need to be more austerely critical in examining abstract language than in examining concrete language.

[1] A tiresome deficiency of the English language is that we have no word corresponding to visualization for the other senses; here I use it to include them.

XII. SUBDIVISIONS

REALISM, ROMANCE AND UNREALITY

Ah! wherefore all this wormy circumstance?
Why linger at the yawning tomb so long?
O for the gentleness of old Romance,
The simple plaining of a minstrel's song!

JOHN KEATS: *Isabella*

IN prose, as in other forms of literature and in other arts, we can fail to appreciate a piece of work and can even sneer at it not because it is bad but because we approach it looking for the wrong things. We should all realize at once that someone who complained that the New Testament was not amusing, that *The Comedy of Errors* lacked profundity or that Poe's *The Pit and the Pendulum* was not a story of usual experience, was being inept. It is not, however, at all uncommon for someone to complain, with exactly the same ineptitude, that the kind of experimental prose that verges on poetry, such as Virginia Woolf's *The Waves*, tells no exciting story; that a novel about the experiences of soldiers in the front line is 'unpleasant'; that Jane Austen contributes nothing to the understanding of the tragic social problems of her day or that William Faulkner is not suitable for the nursery.

Most of us will prefer some types of prose writing to others. I prefer Fielding to Jane Austen, Dickens to Thackeray and Joyce Cary to Angela Thirkell; this no doubt gives some indication of my own personality; but it does not mean that

I am entirely without appreciation of the style of the other authors. One cannot really say that oranges are better than apples or fish better than meat. One can say only that meat is better than synthetic protein coloured pink.

All art is selective. A story or essay will achieve an effect on the reader by the selection of some aspects of the subject. We can choose, if told to write an essay on Eggs, to write a practical, informative essay advising the housewife on the choice, storage and cookery of eggs; we may write as biologists and discuss the different kinds of egg, including fish roe, turtle eggs and the eggs of the duck-billed platypus. We may adopt a more literary manner and write of roc's eggs, the Herne's Egg[1] and the eggs of Leda from which were hatched Helen of Troy, Clytemnestra, Castor and Pollux; or we may choose to be flippant and write about the mishaps that can occur in connection with eggs. One thing about our choice, if we are to write a good essay, is certain; we shall not try to treat of all these aspects of the subject in one essay. The very mood and tone of voice required differs for each subject. Thus the rhythm of the sentences, the length of sentences, the choice of words and even the type of punctuation will be dictated by the selection of theme. The first and most necessary and unbreakable convention of every art is that the artist chooses those aspects of the subject he wishes to treat in detail, ignores or almost ignores everything else, and suits the details of the treatment to the chosen matter.

For example, everyone knows the kind of love story in which no one is ever faced with the problem of earning a living—a problem which occupies most of us for the greater part of our waking hours. Such a story is often completely trashy and unreal; but in a great and sincere love story, too, it might be necessary to leave out references to the ordinary tasks of earning a living and running a home, not because the

[1] In a remarkable play by W. B. Yeats.

author did not recognize their existence, but because this particular story was about the development of a relationship and the gradual mental adjustments of two people in love, and, since this is a complex and difficult subject, there was no room in the book for anything else.

Any reader who doubts this principle of selection may make a simple and quite entertaining test. Try to write down everything you said and did and thought yesterday, from rising in the morning to going to sleep at night. You must exclude nothing. You will soon realize that to do this accurately is impossible; your memory itself is mercifully selective. To do it at all would fill a large volume and would be dull reading. Moreover, though you are probably fairly well-behaved and respectable, you could hardly live through a day without at least thinking something, that in print, would give great offence to the average reader on grounds of seemliness or ethics. We all select constantly in normal conversation.

The realistic and the romantic selections from life are two great divisions of fiction. Later we will look at the miserable and sterile hybrid that I describe as unreality.

Realism attempts to portray things as they are. Because some writers—not all bad writers—avoid certain painful aspects of life such as slums, the horrible side of war, tragic racial problems and injustices, dirt, vermin, most diseases,[1] injuries, mental disorders, perversions and violently controversial political problems, novels and plays dealing with these subjects are often specially described as realistic; another aspect of fiction commonly called realism is the treatment of the physical love of men and women as going beyond kisses in the moonlight.

Among the worst enemies of literature are the Bowdlers and Comstocks, the banners and expurgators, who reject a

[1] Conan Doyle in *Tales of Medical Life* has an amusing discussion of the diseases appropriate to polite fiction.

work of art on the grounds that it is not Nice and who wish to deny to the young information that they usually need sooner than prudes and prigs suppose. Such people are a perpetual nuisance to librarians, authors and educators[1] but somehow miss genuinely salacious literature in their attacks. A writer for such people can get away with almost any false values, cowardice, triviality and callous indifference to real human agonies; it is the moment of truth that gives offence. Occasionally these cowards and bullies succeed in getting a realistic book banned, with the result that a sincere author wins notoriety as a writer of 'smut'—this happened to Lawrence and Joyce—and may suffer mental tortures at this cruel misunderstanding.

However, though the reader will have gathered that I am in sympathy with even the more violent forms of realism and vehemently opposed to almost all censorship, except possibly, for the very young and the mentally sick or unstable, it must be admitted that there is a false realism which is a kind of inverted sentimentality. It is possible to appear to be very bold and frank when we are merely wallowing in the disagreeable with a desire to shock or to pander to low tastes. For example, Zola's *L'Assommoir* is a serious realistic novel on the drink problem; in certain American crime novels the detective is represented as drinking so much whisky that in real life he would be quite unfit to carry out his arduous tasks both physical and mental. There have been 'tough' novels about soldiers who go wenching vulgarly and talk about their sexual conquests brutally; such men do exist and we ought to know about them; but in these regiments there seems to be no young soldier who is longing to return to a loved wife or fiancée and is trying to be faithful to her. There have been

[1] Unofficial censors will go to such lengths as borrowing books from libraries in order to destroy them, mutilating books and victimizing teachers.

novels of the French or Russian Revolution in which all the revolutionaries have been cruel, cynical, vicious thirsters for blood and all the aristocrats have been noble, gallant people in pretty clothes who died heroically or escaped deservedly. Such novels, however much blood, sex and brutal language appears in them, are not realistic, for they are fundamentally untrue to human nature with its assorted personalities and very mixed motives.

To be realistic in the true sense we must have a feeling for truth and a sense of proportion. A baby smiling in a perambulator in the Park, playing with his toes under the almond blossom, is just as real as a victim of atomic bombing with his skin sheeting off and his melted eyes running down his roasted cheeks; to pretend that either is not there is to be a comfortable or uncomfortable ostrich.

To me the society in the novels of Jane Austen is somewhat unreal in what might be called an ethical or perhaps a sociological sense, because I do not value social position and am incompetent in matters of etiquette—here I am trying to be objective about my own subjectivity!—and because these small, closed societies, preoccupied with family alliances, inheritances and the lesser decencies, do not seem to me to be doing much that is worth doing; but Jane Austen is a very realistic writer. Her human beings behave as we know human beings often behave, and their personalities differ greatly. Their conversations have, most of the time, the style of real speech. The realism that is always to be accepted and honoured is any serious and responsible portrayal of some aspect of real life.

Realism is thus in a sense the least selective kind of writing, in that it does not automatically exclude any aspect of life; but, paradoxically, true realism is often very selective, because it has a sense of proportion, and a sense of proportion compels a certain selectiveness. The most unselective good novel ever written was probably James Joyce's *Ulysses*, which is the story of a single day in a man's life, omitting nothing; my edition has 742 pages of text! However, the student of this novel will soon realize that the attempts to represent the man's mental life are, of necessity, conventionalized into various patterns, though not, in the usual sense, conventional; and the parallels with, or perhaps parodies of, the *Odyssey* provide another pattern.

The word *romance* has a complicated history and has now become a somewhat vague word; it nowadays covers the austere and moving narratives of *Morte Darthur*, a worthless unreal love story in a women's magazine, a commercial film in which love has been distorted, a child's trivial lie and, sometimes, a real love affair. The word has been so cheapened by people who lacked discrimination that now to call something a romance is to run the risk that you will be misunderstood as despising it! It seems unlikely that the word can now be restored to specialized meaning and freed from those implications of cheap commercial fiction that have clustered round it; but here I wish to use it to denote a treatment of life different from realism, but still sincere and genuinely artistic. Romance makes its selection in a different frame of mind; realism seeks to give us a knowledge of truth, romance what Sir Herbert Read has called a 'sense of glory'. Malory's *Morte Darthur* is the best English example of pure romance; to write unadulterated romance nowadays, when the spread of scientific knowledge, the development of an enquiring attitude to religion and politics, the increasing complexity and organization of modern life and the disillusionments arising from the aftermath of two world wars have forced us to recognize a complexity of life and a multiplicity of moral and psychological shades of meaning that would have been unintelligible to Malory, is probably impossible.

Genuine romance is certainly not sentimental. It portrays

the life of action and takes the sense of honour as the main-spring of life. We know nowadays that it is possible to have a sense of honour in a bad cause; there is nothing desirable in the heroic Storm Trooper or the suicidal Japanese bomber pilot, or, for that matter, in a view of sexual honour that allows for no dilemmas. The heroes and heroines of romance are magnificent, but not very intelligent; and we need intelligence above all to cope with modern life. Yet as soon as we experience the full shock of personal disloyalty we realize the beauty of loyalty; we have only to see one dishonourable action to learn that honour is a beautiful thing.

In romance the value set upon honour leads to the following values being exalted: heroism in fighting and the habit of never refusing a challenge, even by the supernatural powers (Lancelot goes into the Chapel Perillous); indifference to death and acute sensitivity to reputation; mercy where mercy is appropriate; devoted love to one lady, without the expecttation of reward; effort to bring honour to that lady; a general devotion to all ladies in distress; purity and fidelity in women; loyalty to the group (King Arthur's court—this later develops into patriotism); and loyalty to God as expressed in service to the king and sometimes a religious vow or quest (the Grail).

Perhaps one of the last English authors who tried to write genuine romance was Maurice Hewlett; it is doubtful if he wholly succeeded. The nearest equivalent to romance in modern life is not the sentimental, unreal love story and story of impossible adventure that sometimes goes by the name; it is the high-grade detective story. For in a good detective story the hero (Sherlock Holmes, Peter Wimsey, Hercule Poirot) is eager to right wrongs and takes many risks to do so; he frequently helps damsels in distress and is himself a man of distinguished character and accomplishments. Again, as G. K. Chesterton pointed out, the detective story asks no questions about customary moral values, as the realistic story often does.

Subdivisions, Realism, Romance and Unreality

A mixture of romance and realism is likely to be more popular today than undiluted romance. Helen Waddell's fine novel *Peter Abelard* is a good example of this, and probably the curious and stimulating supernatural thrillers of Charles Williams also come into this category. (Charles Williams's philosophy of life was a romantic theology which gave rise to many fruitful speculations.)

Although the romances of the age of chivalry expressed its highest moral standards, and real romance probably came to an end with the end of feudalism, the romances were not a realistic portrayal of their own times. A reading of history, or indeed merely a little common sense, shows that there was a darker side to this grand code of action and honour; today, in realistic fiction, we choose to show life as it is and not as we feel it ought to be. There is, however, an element of romance in much good realistic literature. We wish to know about life, and we thus appreciate a realistic portrayal of life;[1] but we do also wish to be thrilled and, more important, encouraged, by tales of courage, loyalty and magnanimity—episodes that make us proud to be human. There is nothing unrealistic in portraying such episodes; human beings *can* be very fine.

The limitation of romance is that it is essentially simple; the moral issue involved has to be one of black versus white, which in our present civilization is not a common contrast. The possible solution to the problem is always intellectually simple to perceive, however hard it may be to carry out. On the whole, too, the hero of romance must not be troubled with such questions as legality, planning a career or earning a living; and though he may bleed and die he seldom has catarrh or colic. Thus the modern realistic novel can have

---

[1] This is not entirely true; some people find it impossible to enjoy a realistic presentation of something very remote from their own experience.

episodes of romance without irritating us, for such episodes do occur in real life; but it cannot keep this up for long.

Realism is an attempt at a complete portrayal of reality; romance is a portrayal of one of the more thrilling and inspiring aspects of reality; much bad literature might well be described as unrealism. Unrealism is very popular, for the real 'classics', the great experimental modern novels and even the intelligent psychological or problem novels of today make too many demands on the ignorant, stupid or insensitive reader. The typical 'best-seller' is a book for those who like reading but have never really learned how to read; nowadays it is very nearly literature, but not quite, it is generally very well constructed and written in good English in the common style; its characters are very nearly alive; the difference between trained talent and true genius is obvious only to people who have had a fairly long exposure to genius. An amusing but grim comment on the public fear of realism is to be found often in the pages of the monthly journal of two respectably intelligent middlebrow book clubs, World Books and Reader's Union. Every time a realistic work is a monthly choice the choosers are greeted with a shower of abuse for printing something sordid, and the writers of protest letters frequently boast of having put these books on the fire. It is obvious that in some homes all the worthwhile choices go up the chimney and only the pleasant ephemera remain on the shelves.

The imitation of literature that often masquerades as the real thing is a menace to real literature, because it gives people the impression that great art can be enjoyed without strenuous mental efforts or emotional shocks. Sometimes we feel the need for a little 'escape' reading; the crime novel, the trivial light novel, the scientific fiction, the 'Western', the unscholarly historical novel or the popular magazine may have a function even for intelligent people. When we consider the shortness of life, the amazing interestingness of the world about us and the many useful or interesting things there are to do, we may feel ashamed of reading 'escape' literature; but civilized life presents many painful conflicts and when we feel tired we may find it pardonable to escape into a world of unrealities. What seems to me to be important is that if we are to read trivial literature at all we must learn to differentiate between escape reading and worthwhile reading, between nourishment and narcotics.

It is difficult to define reality in literature, as opposed to unreality, but the difference would seem to be in part artistic, in part psychological or moral—as with subjectivity and objectivity. The moral difference is that for reality we must have sincerity. It is possible to write quite readable stories to a formula; it does not seem to be possible to write great novels without a certain fundamental sense of vocation. Dickens and the Brontës seem to me to be much better writers than Trollope, partly for this reason. Much of the ephemeral literature to be found in magazines is merely commercial, written to a formula, without real emotional experience or moral purpose, or even a passion for artistry, behind it. Dr. Johnson said that no man but a blockhead ever wrote except for money; this was one of his endearingly characteristic oversimplifications; there are some things Dr. Johnson would not have written for any money; and it is probable that no great writer has ever written only for money.

Sincerity, however, is not enough; there must be craftsmanship as well. Unfortunately most of us are still so immature at the end of our days that we can be perfectly sincere in having emotions that are out of all proportion to reality; and it may be true that some writers whose work is notoriously unreal quite honestly believe that life is as they portray it. Most of them, however, probably write tongue-in-cheek.

A fantasy or other highly imaginative piece of work may

be far more realistic than a novel that pretends to be a portrayal of real life. H. G. Well's *The Invisible Man* has an impossible central situation, but the treatment of the situation is realistic; George Orwell's fable *Animal Farm*, although a work very much of the imagination, is a far more realistic and intelligent study of the Russian Revolution and its development than those novels which are interested only in emigré White Russians selling their jewellery.

Here is a somewhat flippant but possibly helpful table of some of the distinctions to be remembered in discriminating among three types of writing:

	REALISM	ROMANCE	UNREALITY
PLOT	Probable in some sense	Possible or supernatural	Plausible and improbable
CHARACTERS	Varying shades of grey tinged with other colours	Black and white	Nearly colourless or colours not fast
	Psychologically convincing	Mythical types	Dull types
SETTING	Very varied and detailed	Some feudal community	Anywhere, inaccurately represented
MORALITY	Exploratory	Carefully conventional	Carelessly conventional
THE READER IDENTIFIES HIMSELF WITH	Characters he could easily be in suitable conditions	Characters he would like to be and would be better as	Characters he would wish to be in his sillier daydreams
THE AUTHOR SEEKS	to explore life	to extol some lofty ideals	to earn some money

THE PROSE STYLE	Clear common or sometimes individual	Usually direct, simple, now archaic	Cheap and nasty
THE SUCCESS	Good sales or moderate for some years, at best as long as romance	Success with a small public for several hundred years	Huge success for a few months

XIII. SUBDIVISIONS

SOME SPECIAL CONVENTIONS

Whate'er the scene, let this advice have weight:
Adapt your language to your hero's state.

BYRON: Hints from Horace

THIS will be a chapter of scraps of information intended to help the student to classify some of the
more unusual kinds of individual style. Before giving
some more terms, I will take the opportunity to explain that
all classification in matters of art is dangerous. This is as true
of poetry, drama, music, painting or sculpture as it is of prose.
We invent and use literary terms so that we can talk about
literature and be intelligible to other people; but the school
child, the student and the inexperienced adult are very apt to
think that these classifications are rules, not mere conven-
iences, and to be vexed whenever a work of art does not come
neatly into some memorized category. It is fatally easy to
learn a list of critical terms and then apply them glibly in
examinations; this is hardly real criticism and often leads to
howlers of a most pathetic kind. However, some loose classifications are useful, not in providing watertight compartments
for different styles—such never-overlapping divisions cannot
be invented—but in helping people to think about prose and
to differentiate styles.

One convention that has been popular for some time is
what might be called the rustic convention. Perhaps it may be

traced back to the eighteenth-century cult of the 'noble savage', the idea, developing as a natural reaction to a distressingly complex society, that country people and savages[1] are people of simple emotions and refreshing folk-wisdom. Later researches have shown that this was a pretty dream; but the rustic convention in literature can be appealing: simple people are portrayed as speaking their own rather naïve, simple and often ungrammatical language, sometimes in actual dialect, and are shown as having a certain homely wisdom or touching sincerity. For instance, in *Precious Bane* Mary Webb speaks through a rustic person in a rustic style, and this heightens the impression of helpless suffering and bewilderment, stressing the strong, primitive emotions and the slow but often fruitful workings of an untrained intellect.

'I loosed Bendigo and the oxen and cows, such as were lying in, and they went pounding away into the woods, half crazy with fear. I woke Mother and told her she must dress and come to the mere and dip while we made a chain for the buckets, to send them from hand to hand. I got together all the pails and buckets, and thought it seemed a pitiful thing that with all the great mere full of water we could only slake our fire with as much as we could get into our little buckets. And I've thought since that when folk grumble about this and that and be not happy, it is not the fault of creation, that is like a vast mere full of good, but it is the fault of their bucket's smallness.'

(Book IV, Chapter 2)

Among earlier novels a very happy use of the rustic convention in style as well as in subject-matter is to be found in *Lorna Doone*, in which the hero, John Ridd, tells his exciting story in his own simple and sometimes clumsy language. From

[1] And, in a slightly different line of thought, young children.

this we are somehow made more able to believe in his sincerity; and the language used itself often throws a good deal of light on the character:

'The upshot of it all was this, that as no Lorna came to me, except in dreams or fancy, and as my life was not worth living without constant sign of her, forth I must again to find her, and say more than a man can tell. Therefore, without waiting longer for the moving of the spring, dressed as I was in grand attire (so far as I had gotten it), and thinking my appearance good, although with doubts about it (being forced to dress in the hay-tallat), round the corner of the wood-stack went I very knowingly—for Lizzie's eyes were wondrous sharp—and thus I was sure of meeting none, who would care or dare to speak of me.

'It lay upon my conscience often, that I had not made dear Annie secret to this history, although in all things I could trust her, and she loved me like a lamb. Many and many a time I tried, and more than once began the thing; but there came a dryness in my throat, and a knocking under the roof of my mouth, and a longing to put it off again, as perhaps might be wisest. And then I would remember too, that I had no right to speak of Lorna, as if she were common property.'

(Chapter XIX)

The rustic convention, which is often used by authors who are themselves highly sophisticated, should not be confused with the more primitive prose of earlier times, when the simplicity and occasionally awkwardness of language was due not to any conscious quest for an appealing flavour of innocence but merely to the lack of a long tradition of prose to serve as models for more polished and complex sentences:

'Hereupon as well the archbishop as the earle marshall submitted themselves unto the king, and to his sonne the lord

John that was there present, and returned not to their armie. Whereupon their troops scaled and fled their waies; but, being pursued, manie were taken, manie slaine, and manie spoiled of that that they had about them, & so permitted to go their waies. Howsoever the matter was handled, true it is that the archbishop, and the earle marshall were brought to Pomfret to the king, who in this meane was advanced thither with his power; and from thence he went to Yorke, whither the prisoners were also brought, and there beheaded the morrow after Whitsuntide in a place without the citie: that is to understand, the archbishop himselfe, the earle marshall, sir John Lampleie, and sir William Plumpton. Unto all which persons, though indemnitie were promised, yet was the same to none of them at anie hand performed.'

HOLINSHED: *The Chronicles of England* (1577)

Another special convention, confined to a fairly short period in history, is known as Euphuism; the name is taken from John Lyly's novel *Euphues* (1578-1580) and the characteristics of the style are a very lavish use of alliteration, a rather sing-song rhythm and the use of a great many similes drawn from natural history or the series of pretty legends that once did duty for natural history. Other similes and rhetorical devices are sprinkled very thickly.

'They uttered nothing to make a man laugh, therefore I will leave them. Mary their outwarde gestures would now and then afford a man a morsel of mirth; of those two I meane not so much, as of all the other traine of opponents and respondents. One peckt with his forefinger at everie halfe sillable hee brought forth, and nodded with his nose like an old singing man, teaching a yong querister to keepe time. Another would be sure to wipe his mouth with his handkercher at the ende of every ful point, and ever when he thought he had cast a figure so curiously, as he dived over head and eares into his auditors admiration, hee would take occasion to stroke up his haire, and twine up his mustachios twice or thrice over while they might have leasure to applaud him. A third wavered and wagled his head, like a proud horse playing with his bridle, or as I have seene some fantasticall swimmer, at everie stroke train his chin sidelong over his left shoulder. A fourth swet and foamed at the mouth, for verie anger his adversarie had denied that part of the sillogisme which he was not prepared to answere. A fifth spread his armes, like an usher that goes before to make rome, and thript with his finger and his thumbe when he thought he had tickled it with a conclusion. A sixt hung down his countenance like a sheepe, and stutted and slavered very pitifully when his invention was stept aside out of the way. A seventh gaspt for winde, and groned in his pronunciation as if hee were hard bound with some bad argument. Grosse plodders they were all, that had some learning and reading, but no wit to make use of it.'

THOMAS NASHE: *The Unfortunate Traveller*

There is an epigrammatic style which runs in separate sentences, each packed with meaning, more obviously than in paragraphs. This is not confined to any one period. Francis Bacon is the best-known example, but here is a passage of this type from another author:

'Our composition must be more accurate in the beginning and end than in the midst; and in the end more than in the beginning; for in the midst the stream bears us. And this is attained by Custom more than care of diligence. We must express readily, and fully, not profusely. There is difference between a liberal and a prodigal hand. As it is a great point of Art, when our matter requires it, to enlarge, and veer out all sail; so to take it in and contract it is of no less praise when the Argument doth ask it. Either of them had their fitness in the place. A good man always profits by his endeavour, by his help; yea, when he is absent; nay, when he is dead by his example and memory. So good Authors in their style: A strict and succinct style is that, where you can take away nothing without loss, and that loss to be manifest.'

BEN JONSON: *Discoveries*

It will not surprise the reader to know that Jonson had a great admiration for Bacon.

There is a contemporary vogue of a Tough Style, especially in some American fiction, not all of it being contemptible. This style is full of slang, often very vivid and picturesque slang, and of racy colloquialisms; the sentences are generally short, partly to give the impression of crowding action and partly to suggest that the speaker (for such narratives are usually in the third person) is a man of action, not a man of many words. Raymond Chandler is a good example of this; Peter Cheyney has used the same mode without Chandler's veiled sense of the dignity and pathos of human life. It could perhaps be argued that this is one variant of the rustic convention.

The style usually known as Stream of Thought or Stream of Consciousness is important in modern fiction. This has already been mentioned briefly in Chapter IV. The most outstanding examples of this in its extreme form, an attempt at an accurate copying of the processes of thought, are the late novels of Virginia Woolf and *Ulysses*; James Joyce's subsequent experiment, *Finnegan's Wake*, is more like a portrayal of the processes of the subconscious mind than the normal processes of conscious thought, and there are, indeed, passages in *Ulysses* of which this is true. Many lesser modern novelists, and many who in other aspects of their work are not experimental or eccentric, use single paragraphs intended to represent thoughts, say of someone in the grip of sexual or revengeful passion, someone falling asleep or someone sitting daydreaming. Examples will be found—together with some interesting commentaries on how far thoughts can be expressed in words—in André Maurois's short novel *The Thought Reading Machine*.[1]

It is often interesting to notice how a writer has imitated other writers; it is well known that Stevenson trained himself by imitating other styles, and the influence of one writer upon another has played a great part in literary history. This passage surely gives evidence of Kingsley's extensive and habitual reading of the Bible, if we examine the rhythm and sentence structure:

'Then Theseus flung him from him, and lifted up his dreadful club; and before Procrustes could strike him he had struck, and felled him to the ground.

'And once again he struck him; and his evil soul fled forth, and went down to Hades squeaking, like a bat into the darkness of a cave.

'Then Theseus stript him of his gold ornaments, and went up to his house, and found there great wealth and treasure, which he had stolen from the passers-by. And he called the people of the country, whom Procrustes had spoiled a long time, and parted the spoil among them, and went down the mountains, and away.

'And he went down the glens of Parnes, through mist, and cloud, and rain, down the slopes of oak, and lentisk, and arbutus, and fragrant bay, till he came to the Vale of Cephisus, and the pleasant town of Aphidnai, and the home of the Phytalid heroes, where they dwelt beneath a mighty elm.

'And there they built an altar, and bade him bathe in Cephisus, and offer a yearling ram, and purified him from the blood of Sinis, and sent him away in peace.

'And he went down the valley by Acharnai, and by the

---

[1] A translation from the French is available.

silver-swirling stream, while all the people blessed him, for the fame of his prowess had spread wide, till he saw the plain of Athens, and the hill where Athene dwells.'

CHARLES KINGSLEY: The Heroes

John Bunyan and many of the sermon-writers of the seventeenth century are even closer imitators of the style of the Authorised Version.

A special stylistic device is one which might usefully be called Fugue. This is the repetition of a word or phrase in slightly different rhythmical and sense contexts in order to emphasize it. With an author who has also an ear for rhythm, this can be magnificent; here is a wonderful piece of rhetorical exaggeration that heightens its effect by such repetition. This fugue in prose might be compared with repetition in poetry.

'I have seen Minute-glasses; Glasses so short-liv'd. If I were to preach upon this Text, to such a glass, it were enough for half a Sermon; enough to show the worldly man his Treasure, and the Object of his heart (*for, where your Treasure is, there will your Heart be also*) to call his eye to that Minute-glass, and to tell him, There flows, there flies your Treasure, and your Heart with it. But if I had a Secular Glass, a Glass that would run an age; if the two Hemispheres of the World were composed in the form of such a Glass and all the World calcin'd and burnt to ashes, and all the ashes, and sands, and atoms of the World put into that Glass, it would not be enough to tell the godly man what his Treasure, and the object of his Heart is.'

JOHN DONNE: a Sermon

Parallelism is another special kind of prose style. We shall, of course, find single parallelisms in many books; we use them every day—'Mary works hard and is very sensible, but Cicely is idle and irresponsible.' There are, however, some pieces of sustained prose composed of nothing but parallelism:

'A wise son maketh a glad father; but a foolish son is the heaviness of his mother.

'Treasures of wickedness profit nothing: but righteousness delivereth from death.

'The Lord will not suffer the souls of the righteous to famish: but He casteth away the substance of the wicked.

'He becometh poor that dealeth with a slack hand: but the hand of the diligent maketh rich.

'He that gathereth in summer is a wise son: but he that sleepeth in harvest is a son that causeth shame.

'Blessings are upon the head of the just: but violence covereth the mouth of the wicked.

'The memory of the just is blessed: but the name of the wicked shall rot.'

Proverbs 10: 1-7

Some styles are very allusive and to appreciate them to the full requires a wide reading and plenty of general knowledge. In poetry Milton is probably the supreme English example of this. Here is an example in prose.

'O Wickliff, Luther, Hampden, Sidney, Somers, mistaken Whigs and thoughtless Reformers in religion and politics, and all ye, whether poets or philosophers, heroes or sages, inventors of arts or sciences, patriots, benefactors of the human race, enlighteners and civilizers of the world, who have (so far) reduced opinion to reason, and power to law, who are the cause that we no longer burn witches and heretics at slow fires, that the thumb-screws are no longer applied by ghastly, smiling judges, to extort confession of imputed crimes from sufferers for conscience sake: that men are no longer strung up like acorns on trees without judge or jury, or hunted like wild beasts through thickets and glens: who have abated the cruelty of priests, the pride of nobles, the divinity of kings in former times: to whom we owe it that we no longer wear round our necks the collar of Gurth the swineherd and of Wamba the jester, that the castles of great lords are no longer the dens of banditti, whence they issue with fire and sword to lay waste the land, that we no longer expire in loathsome dungeons without knowing the cause, or have our right hands struck off for raising them in self-defence against wanton insult, that we can sleep without fear of being burnt in our beds, or travel without making our wills: that no Amy Robsarts are thrown down trapdoors by Richard Varneys with impunity, that no Red Reiver of Westburn-Flat sets fire to peaceful cottages, that no Claverhouse signs cold-blooded death-warrants in sport, that we have no Tristan L'Hermite or Petit-André, crawling near us like spiders, and making our flesh creep, and our hearts sicken within us at every moment of our lives—ye, who have produced this change in the face of nature and society, return to earth once more, and beg pardon of Sir Walter and his patrons, who sigh at not being able to undo all that you have done!'

WILLIAM HAZLITT: *The Spirit of the Age*

Hazlitt admired Scott as a novelist but disliked his reactionary politics; and much of the sarcastic force of this passage is given by the fact that most of the allusions to the grim 'good old days' are taken from Scott's own novels.

Sometimes it may be illuminating to consider whether vividiness is achieved by a wealth of actual detail giving us a clear picture:

'Estimating the size of the creature by comparison with the diameter of the large trees near which it passed—the few giants of the forest which had escaped the fury of the landslide—I concluded it to be far larger than any ship of the line in existence. I say ship of the line, because the shape of the monster suggested the idea—the hull of one of our seventy-fours might convey a very tolerable conception of the general outline. The mouth of the animal was situated at the extremity of a proboscis some sixty or seventy feet in length, and about as thick as the body of an ordinary elephant. Near the root of this trunk was an immense quantity of black shaggy hair—more than could have been supplied by the coats of a score of buffaloes; and projecting from this hair downwardly and laterally, sprang two gleaming tusks not unlike those of the wild boar, but of infinitely greater dimension. Extending forward, parallel with the proboscis, and on each side of it, was a gigantic staff, thirty or forty feet in length, formed seemingly of pure crystal, and in shape a perfect prism:—it reflected in the most gorgeous manner the rays of the declining sun. The trunk was fashioned like a wedge with the apex to the earth. From it there were outspread two pairs of wings—each wing nearly one hundred yards in length—one pair being placed above the other, and all thickly covered with metal scales; each scale apparently some ten or twelve feet in diameter. I observed that the upper and lower tiers of wings were connected by a strong chain. But the chief peculiarity of this horrible thing, was the representation of a *Death's Head*, which covered nearly the whole surface of its breast, and which was as accurately traced in glaring white, upon the dark ground of the body, as if it had been there carefully designed by an artist.'

EDGAR ALLEN POE: *Tales of Mystery and Imagination*

or whether it is achieved by an accumulation of lively fancies and figures:

'*Falstaff:* Have I lived to be carried in a basket, and to be thrown into the Thames like a barrow of butcher's offal? Well, if I be served such another trick, I'll have my brains ta'en out, and buttered, and give them to a dog for a new year's gift. The rogues slighted me into the river with as little remorse as they would have drowned a blind bitch's puppies, fifteen in the litter, and you may know by my size that I have a kind of alacrity in sinking: if the bottom were as deep as hell, I should down. I had been drowned but that the shore was shelvy and shallow; a death that I abhor, for the water swells a man, and what a thing should I have been when I had been swelled! I should have been a mountain of mummy.'

SHAKESPEARE: *The Merry Wives of Windsor*, III, 5

In a sense it could be argued that the style of every individual author is his or her own separate convention, if the style is at all individual. It is often worth while to look out for the favourite words, the favourite sentence structures, the favourite rhythms and the favourite figures of speech of a particular author.

An aspect of prose style which may conveniently be mentioned in this chapter of scraps is the matter of prose translation. This is fairly important, for French and Russian novels, especially, are widely read in translation and translations from many other languages are among the books known to the cultured English reader. The test of a translation is, roughly: first, does it convey all the meaning and as much as possible of the style of the original? secondly, does it read sufficiently like an original work to spare us the irritation of continually wondering whether the translator or the original is to blame for some awkwardness of style? Styles in translations will thus differ as much as styles in the original language or in the language of the translation; and a translation is not necessarily without merit as, in itself, a work of literature; the Authorised Version of the Bible is a translation, and I have been told that some French readers prefer to read Proust in Scott-Moncrieff's translation.

XIV. SUBDIVISIONS

PROSE FOR ITS OWN SAKE

The only excuse for making a useless thing is that one admires it
intensely.

OSCAR WILDE

I N all prose writing style should have some importance;
but in most prose writing content is more important
than style.

There is a purely functional prose, the prose of instructions,
text-books, encyclopaedias, reports and so on. Most of the
prose the ordinary person reads for relaxation will be fiction;
in this the story and characters provide the main interest; often
we do not notice the style of a novel when we are reading it,
unless it is so unusual as to demand our special concentration
or so slovenly as to vex us.

At a fairly late stage in history[1] there comes a small class of
literature in which content is quite unimportant and the style
itself is the very reason for writing. In the eighteenth century
essays were usually either informative or moral, though the
moral purpose was not necessarily the inculcation of important virtues and might be merely the correction of some
deviation from taste or good manners. In the nineteenth
century such writers as Charles Lamb and Leigh Hunt wrote
some essays on very trivial topics for, as it seems, the sheer joy

---

[1] Perhaps the recent growth of 'abstract art' is a parallel?

of playing with those topics in admirably polished and individual prose.

'I had no repugnance then—why should I now have?—to those little, lawless, azure-tinctured grotesques, that under the notion of men and women, float about, uncircumscribed by any element, in that world before perspective—a china teacup.

'I like to see my old friends—whom distance cannot diminish—figuring up in the air (so they appear to our optics), yet on *terra firma* still—for so we must in courtesy interpret that speck of deeper blue—which the decorous artist, to prevent absurdity, had made to spring up beneath their sandals.

'I love the men with women's faces, and the women, if possible, with still more womanish expressions.

'Here is a young and courtly Mandarin, handing tea to a lady from a salver—two miles off. See how distance seems to set off respect! And here the same lady, or another—for likeness is identity on tea-cups—is stepping into a little fairy boat, moored on the hither side of this calm garden river, with a dainty mincing foot, which in a right angle of incidence (as angles go in our world) must infallibly land her in a flowery mead—a furlong off on the other side of the same strange stream!

'Farther on—if far or near can be predicated of their world —see horses, trees, pagodas, dancing the hays.

'Here—a cow and rabbit couchant, and co-extensive—so objects show, seen through the lucid atmosphere of fine Cathay.'

CHARLES LAMB: *Old China*

More recent writers whose prose—usually, though not invariably, in the form of the essay—has been this prose for its own sake, this luxurious splashing in a frothy and tempting style, include Max Beerbohm, Robert Lynd, Rose Macaulay,

G. K. Chesterton, Hilaire Belloc and Paul Jennings; not all of these are always in this mood.

'Childhood has always seemed to me to be the tragic period of life. To be subject to the most odious espionage at the one age when you never dream of doing wrong, to be deceived by your parents, thwarted of your smallest wish, oppressed by the terrors of manhood and of the world to come, and to believe, as you are told, that childhood is the only happiness known; all this is quite terrible.'

MAX BEERBOHM: *King George the Fourth* (*Works*)

Many very serious books, both factual and fictional, have been written on the subject of childhood; and it is difficult to keep all emotion out of any reference to so profoundly painful and complicated a theme; for a moment we could almost think that this paragraph was serious in intent; but the urbane 'quite' gives it the necessary flavour of frivolity. It is a clever trick of vocabulary and rhythm to give urbanity and lightness to what could easily become tragic and bitter. Here is the same polished precision and astonishing deftness applied to a subject no one would be tempted to take seriously:

'Surely the common prejudice against painting the lily can but be based on mere ground of economy. That which is already fair is complete, it may be urged—urged implausibly, for there are not so many lovely things in the world that we can afford not to know each one of them by heart. There is only one white lily, and who that has ever seen—as I have—a lily really well painted could grudge the artist so fair a ground for his skill?'

MAX BEERBOHM: *The Pervasion of Rouge* (*Works*)

It is also possible for a narrative to be trivial in matter and for most of the delight in reading it to come from the manner of the telling. Here the mock-pomposity of some of the vocabulary helps to enliven an account of a trivial episode told in a letter to a friend; good letter-writers, indeed, frequently cultivate prose style for its own sake in order to amuse and please their friends.

'It is a sort of paradox, but it is true: we are never more in danger than when we think ourselves most secure, nor in reality more secure than when we seem to be most in danger. Both sides of this apparent contradiction were lately verified by my experience.—Passing from the greenhouse to the barn, I saw three kittens (for we have so many in our retinue) looking with fixed attention at something, which lay on the threshold of a door, coiled up. I took but little notice of them at first; but a loud hiss engaged me to attend more closely, when behold—a viper! the largest I remember to have seen, rearing itself, darting its forked tongue, and ejaculating the afore-mentioned hiss at the nose of a kitten almost in contact with his lips. I ran into the hall for a hoe with a long handle, with which I intended to assail him, and returning in a few seconds missed him: he was gone, and I feared had escaped me. Still however the kitten sat watching immoveably upon the same spot. I concluded, therefore, that, sliding between the door and the treshold, he had found his way out of the garden into the yard. I went round immediately, and there found him in close conversation with the old cat, whose curiosity being excited by so novel an appearance, inclined her to pat his head repeatedly with her fore foot; with her claws however sheathed, and not in anger; but in the way of philosophical enquiry and examination. To prevent her falling a victim to so laudable an exercise of her talents, I interposed in a moment with the hoe, and performed upon him an act of decapitation, which though not immediately mortal, proved so in the end.'

WILLIAM COWPER

Cowper enjoyed this little tale so much that he versified it, keeping very close to the details given here, in a little mock-heroic poem, *The Colubriad*.

Many books that are predominantly what might be called functional prose, that is, prose in which the content is more important than the style, will have passages of this kind; Henry Fielding, Charles Reade, Jane Austen, Charles Dickens, for example, have passages of this playful technique; and Sterne's *Tristram Shandy* is a novel in which style is all-important as well as being highly individual; to read this book for the story would be unbearable.

XV. THE HISTORICAL
APPROACH

You do not expect me, and you will not hear
In my cadences a voice you recognise.
You will not be glad to meet William Shakespeare
Himself, though you may have read his tragedies.

NICHOLAS MOORE: *The Return of William Shakespeare*

T HE study of prose, like the study of any other art, is
made more interesting and often more intelligible
by some idea of the history of the art. The reader
who has no knowledge of this whatever may mistake for a
queer, very personal style what was in fact the common style
of the period, or may make fatuous comments on such things
as unusual spellings. Let us look at some fairly typical pieces of
prose from different periods, though bearing in mind that
there is no such thing as the typical style of a period; all the
greatest writers have individual characteristics. Old English
prose will be excluded; it is a separate language.

'And Jesus seeing the people, went up in to an hill, and when
he was set, his disciples camen to him, and he opened his
mouth and taught them and said; Blessed be poor men in
spirit: for the kingdom of heaven is theirn. Blessed be mild
men: for they shall weeld the earth. Blessed be they that
mournen: for they shallen be comforted. Blessed be they that
hungren and thirsten (for) righteousness: for they shallen be
fulfilled. Blessed be merciful men: for they shallen get mercy.

Blessed be they that be of clean heart: for they shallen see God. Blessed be peacable men: for they shallen be clepid Goddes children. Blessed be they that suffren persecution for right-eousness: for the kingdom of heaven is theirn. Ye shallen be blessed when men shallen curse you and shallen pursue you, and shallen say all evil against you lying for me. Joy ye and be glad, for your mede is plenteous in heaven, for so they han pursued prophets that weren also before you.'

Wycliffe's Translation of the Bible (fourteenth century)

The reader may care to compare this with the Authorised Version of the Beatitudes. Here we still have verb endings and a few other words or word forms no longer used in English today; this is really a matter of the history of the language, not of style. The impression is very much that of the strange and archaic, though perfectly comprehensible. The rhythms are less impressive than those of the Authorised Version.

'Right so Sir Lancelot departed, and when he came unto the chapel perilous he alight down, and tied his horse to a little gate. And as soon as he was within the churchyard he saw on the front of the chapel many fair rich shields turned up so down, and many of the shields Sir Lancelot had seen knights bear beforehand. With that he saw by him stand there a thirty great knights, more by a yard than any man that ever he had seen, and all those grinned and gnashed at Sir Lancelot. And when he saw their countenance he dread him sore, and so put his shield afore him, and took his sword in his hand ready unto battle; and they were all armed in black harness, ready with their shields and their swords drawn. And when Sir Lancelot would have gone through them, they scattered on every side of him, and gave him the way, and therewith he waxed all bold and entered into the chapel, and then he saw no light but a dim lamp burning, and then was he ware of a corpse covered with a cloth of silk.'

SIR THOMAS MALORY: *Morte Darthur*, VI, 15

(fifteenth century)

Here we may notice the directness and simplicity of the language; the sensitivity to rhythm; the dignity and the ornamental use of alliteration that is so delicate we hardly notice it in ordinary reading.

'Not long after our sitting down, "I have strange news brought me," saith Mr. Secretary, "this morning, that divers scholars of Eton be run away from the school, for fear of beating." Whereupon Mr. Secretary took occasion to wish that some more discretion were in many schoolmasters in using correction, than commonly there is. Who many times punish rather the weakness of nature, than the fault of the scholar. Whereby many scholars, that might else prove well, be driven to hate learning, before they know what learning meaneth: and so are made willing to forsake their book and be glad to be put to any other kind of living.'

ROGER ASCHAM: *The Schoolmaster* (sixteenth century)

This is a simple style, and might, perhaps, be taken as an example of the common style of the sixteenth century; but this was also an age of much conscious experiment in prose and Euphuism, already mentioned, was one of the favourite styles of the period. Here is another example even more ornate than that already quoted:

'But alasse, I see everie prosperous puffe hath his boisterous blaste, everie sweete hath his sower, everie weale his woe, everie gale of good lucke, his storme of sinister fortune: yea, everie commoditie his discommoditie annexed: the bloud of the Viper is most healthfull for the sight, and most hurtfull for the stomacke, the stone Celonites is verie precious for the backe, and very perillous to the braine: the flower of India pleasant to be seene, but whoso smelleth to it, feeleth present smart: so as the joye of her presence procureth my delight, the annoie of her absence breedeth my despight: yea, the feare that she will not repaie my love with liking, and my fancie with affection, that she will not consent to my request, but rather meanes to stiffle mee with the raging stormes of repulse, and daunt me with the doom of deadly denialls, so fretteth my hapless minde with hellish furie, that no plague, no paine, no torment, no torture can worse molest mee, than to bee distressed with this dreadfull despaire.'

ROBERT GREENE: *The Carde of Fancie* (sixteenth century)

'No man can justly censure or condemn another, because indeed no man truly knows another. This I perceive in myself; for I am in the dark to all the world, and my dearest friends behold me but in a cloud. Those that know me but superficially, think less of me than I do of myself; those of my neer acquaintance think more; GOD, Who truly knows me, knows that I am nothing; for He only beholds me and all the world, who looks not on us through a derived ray, or a trajection of a sensible species, but beholds the substance without the helps of accidents, and the forms of things as we their operations. Further, no man can judge another, because no man knows himself: for we censure others but as they disagree from that humour which we fancy laudable in ourselves, and commend others but for that wherein they seem to quadrate and consent with us. So that, in conclusion, all is but that we all condemn. Self-love.'

SIR THOMAS BROWNE: *Religio Medici* (seventeenth century)

Here is an individual style that achieves its individuality by much more mature techniques than the easily imitable tricks of Euphuism. Several other writers of the seventeenth century, for example Donne, Burton, Hooker and Walton, wrote very ornate though definably individual styles; but there was also plenty of simpler writing; here is a less decorative, but very pleasing, style of approximately the same period. It comes rather nearer to common style.

'It is a hard and nice subject for a man to write of himself; it grates his own heart to say anything of disparagement and the reader's ears to hear anything of praise for him. There is no danger from me of offending him in this kind; neither my mind, nor my body, nor my fortune allow me any materials for that vanity. It is sufficient for my own contentment that they have preserved me from being scandalous, or remarkable on the defective side. But besides that, I shall here speak of myself only in relation to the subject of these precedent discourses, and shall be likelier thereby to fall into the contempt than rise up to the estimation of most people. As far as my memory can return back into my past life, before I knew or was capable of guessing what the world, or glories or business of it were the natural affections of my soul gave me a secret bent of aversion from them, as some plants are said to turn away from others, by an antipathy imperceptible to themselves and inscrutable to man's understanding.'

ABRAHAM COWLEY: *Of Myself*

The eighteenth century has been called an age of prose, and its great prose writers all have their marked individual styles, though often with a curious similarity of rhythm; this period greatly favoured the antithetical sentence. Here is a sample of the prose of the greatest orator of the period, as fine for its actual content as for its dignity and vigour.

'We are indeed, in all disputes with the colonies, by the necessity of things, the judges. It is true, sir. But I confess, that the character of judge in my own cause is a thing that frightens me. Instead of filling me with pride, I am exceedingly

humbled by it.[1] I cannot proceed with a stern, assured, judical
confidence, until I find myself in something more like a
judicial character. I must have these hesitations as long as I am
compelled to recollect, that, in my little reading upon such
contests as these, the sense of mankind has, at lease, as often
decided against the superior as the subordinate power. Sir, let
me add too, that the opinion of having some abstract right in
my favour would not put me much at my ease in passing
sentence; unless I could be sure, that there were no rights
which, in their exercise under certain circumstances, were not
the most odious of all wrongs, and the most vexatious of all
injustices. Sir, these considerations have great weight with me,
when I find things so circumstanced, that I see the same party,
at once a civil litigant against me in point of right, and a
culprit before me; while I sit as criminal judge, on acts of his,
whose moral quality is to be decided upon the merits of that
very litigation. Men are every now and then put, by the complexity of human affairs, into strange situations; but justice is
the same, let the judge be in what situation he will.'

EDMUND BURKE: *On Conciliation with America*

Burke is, indeed, one of the more ornate stylists of this
period, in which simplicity and clarity were often regarded as
principal merits, though to the seventeenth century he would
have seemed simple. In the nineteenth century, with the
Romantic Movement,[2] there was something of a reaction in
favour of ornateness. Here, first, is an ornate style applied to a
light-hearted topic.

[1] Strictly this is an ungrammatical and illogical sentence; but in
speech the want of logic would probably pass unnoticed.

[2] This term is a tiresome one. Poets as diverse and often hostile to
one another as Byron, Wordsworth and Keats cannot truly be said to
be a movement. However, everyone knows the meaning of the expression.

'In these assassinations of princes and statesmen, there is nothing to excite our wonder: important changes often depend on their deaths; and from the eminence on which they stand, they are peculiarly exposed to the aim of every artist who happens to be possessed by the craving for scenical effect. But there is another class of assassinations, which has prevailed from an early period of the seventeenth century, that really *does* surprise me; I mean the assassination of philosophers. For, gentlemen, it is a fact, that every philosopher of eminence for the last two centuries has either been murdered, or, at the least, been very near it; insomuch, that if a man calls himself a philosopher, and never had his life attempted, rest assured there is nothing in him; and against Locke's philosophy in particular, I think it an unanswerable objection (if we needed any) that, although he carried his throat about with him in this world for seventy-two years, no man ever condescended to cut it.'

DE QUINCEY: *On Murder Considered as one of the Fine Arts*

The use of an ornate style here might perhaps be called ironical; it is used to impart an air of solemn and academic seriousness to the frivolous theme. Shelley uses an ornate and somewhat high-flown style to emphasize his solemnity in writing on a serious subject.

'The picture is not barren of instruction to actual men. The Poet's self-centred seclusion was avenged by the furies of an irresistible passion pursuing him to speedy ruin. But that Power which strikes the luminaries of the world with sudden darkness and extinction, by awakening them to too exquisite a perception of its influences, dooms to a slow and poisonous death those meaner spirits that dare to abjure its dominion. Their destiny is more abject and inglorious as their delinquency is more contemptible and pernicious. They who, deluded by no generous error, instigated by no sacred thirst, of doubtful knowledge, duped by no illustrious superstition, loving nothing on this earth, and cherishing no hopes beyond, yet keep aloof from sympathies with their kind, rejoicing neither in human joy nor mourning with human grief; these, and such as they, have their apportioned curse. They languish, because none feel with them their common nature. They are morally dead. They are neither friends, nor lovers, nor fathers, nor citizens of the world, nor benefactors of their country. Among those who attempt to exist without human sympathy, the pure and tender-hearted perish through the intensity and passion of their search after its communities, when the vacancy of their spirit suddenly makes itself felt. All else, selfish, blind, and torpid, are those unforeseeing multitudes who constitute, together with their own, the lasting misery and loneliness of the world. Those who love not their fellow-beings live unfruitful lives, and prepare for their old age a miserable grave.'

P. B. SHELLEY: *Preface to Alastor*

This is the image of an eager, passionate and passionately moral personality.

The later nineteenth century had much very ornate prose, notably that of Carlyle and Ruskin, as well as the classicism of Matthew Arnold; and it was a great age of the novel. Here, since some of the novelists have already been quoted, is a passage from a political speech; its ironical twist of surprise is refreshing.

'I appeal to the courage of this nation. How is the English nation as to courage? I will give you my opinion. For real dangers the people of England and Scotland form perhaps the bravest people in the world. At any rate, there is no people in the world to whom they are prepared to surrender or to whom one would ask them to surrender the palm of bravery. But I am sorry to say there is another aspect of the case, and for imaginary dangers there is no people in the world who in a degree anything like the English is the victim of absurd and idle fancies. It is notorious all over the world. The French, we think, are excitable people; but the French stand by in amazement at the passion of fear and fury into which an Englishman will get himself when he is dealing with an imaginary danger.'

W. E. GLADSTONE: *The Irish Question*

Examples of twentieth-century experimental prose have already been given; lest the student should think that all good twentieth-century prose is experimental, a specimen shall be taken from the work of one of the many good contemporary writers who use a more or less traditional style.

' "We must be running late," the passengers had been saying from time to time, uncertainly glancing at one another as though the feeling of lateness might be subjective, then at the blinded windows of the carriage. "Whereabouts would we be now?—how far are we along?" Now and then somebody in a corner prised at a blind's edge, put an eye to the crack—but it was useless; Midland canals and hedges were long gone from view; not a hill or tower showed through the drape of night; every main-line landmark was blotted out. Only a loud catastrophic roar told them, even, when they were in a tunnel. But by now speed had begun to slacken; from the sound of the train, more and more often constricted deep in cuttings between and under walls, they must be entering London: no other city's built-up density could be so strongly felt. Now, with what felt like the timidity of an intruder, the train crept, jarred nervily, came to halts with steam up—allowing traffic over the metal bridges and shunting on wastes of lines to be heard. Passengers who had not yet reached down their bags from the racks now shot up and did so: Stella was among them. The fatigue of the long day's journey had, while it numbed her body into a trance, reduced her mind to one single thought: she was fixed upon what she meant to say. Her hope that Robert would come to meet her had become the hope that she might speak soon.'

ELIZABETH BOWEN: *The Heat of the Day*

Here may be noticed a feature that is very common in the best of the novelists of our own times, the attempt at an almost scientifically accurate description of physical sensations. This may look easy until the reader tries to do it. A few of the other modern novelists who excel in this are Graham Greene, Aldous Huxley, Alex Comfort, Emma Smith, Evelyn Waugh and sometimes C. S. Forester.

To conclude this very small selection of extracts from the prose of different periods, a selection which no one should for a moment take as being adequately representative, a short specimen of prose as experimental and unusual as prose can be without becoming unintelligible is worthy of close study. Puns, compound words carrying a heavy load of multiple meaning, foreign words, hypnotic rhythm and complicated patterns of association are the stylistic devices in a prose which is more like poetry than like traditional prose.

'As my explanations here are probably above your understandings, lattlebrattons, though as augmentatively uncomparisoned as Cadwan, Cadwallan and Cadwalloner, I shall revert to a more expletive method which I frequently use when I have to sermo with muddle crass pupils. Imagine for my purpose that you are a squad of urchins, snifflynosed, goslingnecked, clothyheaded, tangled in your lacings, tingled in your pants, etsiteraw etcicero. And you, Bruno Nowlan, take your tongue out of your inkpot! As none of you knows javanese I will give all my easyfree translation out of the old fabulist's parable. Allaboy Minor, take your head out of your satchel! *Audi*, Joe Peters! *Exaudi* facts!

'The Mookse and the Gripes.

'Gentes and laitymen, fullstoppers and semicolonials, hybreds and lubberds!

'Eins within a space and a wearywide space it wast ere wohned a Mookse. The onesomeness was alltolonely, archunsitlike, broady oval, and a Mookse he would a walking go (My hood! cries Antony Romeo) so one grandsumer evening after a great morning and his good supper of gammon and spittish, having flabelled his eyes, pilleoled his nostrils, vacticanated his ears and palliumed his throats, he put on his impermeable, seized his impugnable, harped on his crown and stepped out of his immobile *De Rure Albo* (socolled because it was chalkfull of masterplasters and had gorgeously letout gardens strown with cascadas, pintacostas, horthoducts and currycombs) and set off from Ludstown *a spasso* to see how badness was badness in the weirdest of all pensible ways.'

JAMES JOYCE: *Finnegans Wake*

This is not mere gibberish. If we trace the various puns and queer inventions to their sources, or even if we relax, sit back and enjoy the rhythm and associations, we realize that such writing is clever, sincere and even delightful, at least in small doses. It has its own kind of wit and eloquence.

The serious student, when examining prose in its historical setting, may find it helpful to remember three facts;

1. Literary history is full of action and reaction; for instance, a period of very ornate prose may be followed by a reaction in favour of extreme simplicity, a cult of sophistication by a cult of naïveté and so on. But it is always dangerous to speak of 'trends' unless we remember that several 'trends' may be at work in the same period, affecting different groups of people.

2. Writers, and perhaps great writers even more than minor ones, often find themselves out of harmony with their own times.

3. Experimentalism, the seeking of a new way of saying things, and traditionalism, the adherence to old ways of saying things, will always at any given moment be found side by side; and both are necessary to the vitality of an art, though experiment usually needs and deserves more deliberate encouragement, since we find it easy to read traditionalist work. The side to which we lean in this continuous battle will always depend a little on age and a great deal on personal temperament; but all experiments grow out of traditions just as all traditional styles were born by experiment; some experiments are failures or dead-ends, but traditions can become exhausted.

XVI. THE SCIENCE OF RHETORIC

Now of Figures. A figure is a certaine decking of speach, whereby the usual and simple fashion thereof is altered and changed to that which is more elegant and conceipted.

ABRAHAM FRAUNCE: *The Arcadian Rhetoric* (1588)

METAPHOR is almost an essential of poetry; prose can be devoid of figures of speech. An account of experimental proof that metals expand when heated, a report on the conduct of a child or a request for a few days' leave from work will be written in straightforward, unadorned language. It is even possible to tell quite a long story with no figures of speech. It is almost impossible to discuss emotion for any length of time without figurative language—anything other than figurative language could be very little more than a scientific account of our secretions and the changes in the brain cells!

What is rhetoric? A few words must here suffice. Rhetoric originally meant the art of persuasion, and was recognized early as a science for which rules could be provided. The first full textbook was Aristotle's *Rhetoric* (322-320 B.C.). In the Roman civilization Cicero and Quintilian wrote important books on the subject and a number of lesser Greek and Roman theorists contributed to the subject. At first it included both valid reasoning, later distinguished as *logic*, and the tricks used in argument; it has gradually come to mean mostly the tricks.

Nowadays it is often regarded almost as the antonym of logic.

In the Middle Ages university students spent their first four years studying grammar, logic and rhetoric, which were thought of as three of the seven liberal arts, the others being music, geometry, arithmetic and astronomy. In these studies, of course, Latin, not the vernacular, was the language of education.

The feeling that, even in prose, the more rhetorical devices the better seems to have continued until fairly late in the seventeenth century—the reader will have found plenty of examples in this book already—when there was a reaction in favour of a 'Close, naked, natural way of speaking'—a demand recorded by Thomas Sprat in his history of the Royal Society. Possibly this reaction against decoration had something to do with Puritanism, but Milton, the greatest Puritan, was a very ornate stylist in both poetry and prose. In the eighteenth century the cult of the simple, direct style continued, but rhetoric, which seems to be in part a natural, spontaneous impulse, as may often be observed in the language of people under the stress of some strong emotion, came back into favour; Burke and Sheridan were celebrated for their eloquence in public debate; and in the nineteenth century rhetoric was again much admired.

At present the general climate of opinion seems to be anti-rhetorical. This is perhaps due in part to one of those action-reaction swings of the pendulum that are inevitable in literary history; perhaps in part it is due to the disillusionment after two major wars and the feeling that rhetoric was merely a device by which politicians could induce young men to go and be killed. However, it may be that we are using a different set of rhetorical devices, that the modern author prefers irony to repetition and understatement to hyperbole. Some modern critics have become so distrustful of rhetoric that they some-times mistake for rant what may well be the genuine expression of violent emotion; it may be the actual emotions that are out of proportion, not the language applied to them.

Many people use rhetorical devices without being aware of the fact. Suppose that someone admires Paul rather than John, whom I admire, and I say indignantly, 'Why, John is worth fifty times as much as Paul, any day!' it is fairly certain that I said what first came into my head and did not think, 'I need a hyperbole for emphasis here.' If I say crossly to an untidy friend, 'You have made a mash and a mess of my papers.' I am not deliberately using alliteration; language tends to come out of the mouth like that.

There is an ethics of rhetoric. Much modern political speaking, advertising and publicity matter makes unscrupulous use of rhetorical devices to arouse emotions that are out of proportion to the subject or are themselves undesirable. On the other hand, a figure of speech may serve to explain something obscure, bring comfort to someone in distress or soften something disagreeable. Rhetorical devices are justifiable when they make truth plainer, arouse desirable emotions and help good purposes, but rhetoric is contemptible and evil when it is misapplied to obscure the truth, spread untruth or incite to wrong actions and poisoned emotions. Rhetoric by itself, like the power derived from atomic fission, is neither good nor bad; it can be used wisely or wrongly. Alas, it may be clever and beautiful whether its purpose is good or bad; and the ethical problem has sometimes been confused with the aesthetic problem, thus contributing to the fashionable disdain for rhetoric.

The rest of this chapter will, on the assumption that no one reading this book wishes to use rhetoric for evil purposes, consist of an account of the rhetorical devices, the figures of speech, in use in English prose. Most of these devices are used in poetry as well.

At this point the inexperienced reader must be reconciled to the task of learning a large number of words that are difficult to spell and odd in appearance. There is a reason for this. The values of a classical education have often been extolled, and the extollers certainly have a strong case; but there are times when I am tempted to suspect that the classical background of English culture has been the curse of English literary criticism.

We have taken our terms of poetic scansion from the Greek, with the result that they do not perfectly fit the genius of our own language and that several good poets have wasted time trying to write English quantitative verse. We have taken most of our grammatical terms from Greek and Latin, again with the result that they do not fit our type of language, for the classical languages are highly inflected and ours is not. This makes grammar, at least as it is still often taught, much more difficult than it need be. We listened to Aristotle on the dramatic unities and spent several generations of dramatic criticism apologizing for Shakespeare as an inspired idiot. In the study of rhetoric, too, we have borrowed a great many terms from Latin and Greek, and thus we have terms for many devices not common in English, such as zeugma and hendiadys, and no universally accepted terms for several devices common in our own language, such as the device I called fugue a little earlier.

It is not surprising that the first English books on the subject, when there was quite a spate of them in the sixteenth century,[1] should have borrowed very heavily from the classical terminologies, for this interest in rhetoric was a result of the Revival of Learning. The student who has to struggle with the list of figures of speech at the end of the grammar book may be surprised to know that most of them were already in use in Shakespeare's day, and may also be

[1] Some of these are: Puttenham, Arte of English Poesie (1589)— still readable; Wilson, Art of Rhetorique (1553); Fraunce, The Arcadian Rhetoric (1588).

The Science of Rhetoric

somewhat consoled to know that the early critics had to learn such terms as *Epanorthosis, Anadiplosis, Epiphonema* and *Proso-popoeia*, to which more homely and spellable names are now given. However, the terminology must now be faced.

1. *Metaphor*

Most people know roughly what a Metaphor is; it is the most important figure of speech, and the commonest. Even in the most ordinary conversation we often use metaphors without knowing that we do so: 'You are a donkey!' 'I am in the soup.' 'We shall have to wait for that till our ship comes in.' Metaphor is that figure of speech in which one thing (or idea, place, person, deed and so forth) is compared to another, without acknowledging in a form of words ('Like', 'as', 'as if', 'even as' . . .) that any comparison is being made.

> 'My Love is *like a red, red rose*'   is a simile, but
> 'For nothing this wide universe I call
> Save thou, *my Rose*'   is a metaphor
> 'Boys and girls tumbling in the street, and playing,
> were *moving jewels*.'
>
> THOMAS TRAHERNE: *Centuries of Meditation*

2. *Simile*

A simile is very like a metaphor, in that it makes a comparison, but in a simile we use a word, generally 'like' or 'as', to show that it is a comparison. This figure too is common in ordinary speech, many similes have become clichés: 'He is as fit as a fiddle'; 'The cat is as black as ink and as fat as butter'; 'He drinks like a fish'. A simile may be used in order to make something clearer or merely as an ornament.

> 'You will be overwhelmed, like *Tarpeia*, by the heavy wealth which you have extracted from tributary generations.'
>
> NEWMAN: *The Scope and Nature of University Education*

'In the distance beyond the blue waters of the lake, and nearly screened by intervening foliage, was seen a shining speck, the rival capital of Tezcuco, and, still further on, the dark belt of porphyry, girdling the valley around *like a rich setting which Nature had devised for the fairest of her jewels.*'

PRESCOTT: *History of the Conquest of Mexico*

In poetry there are often long, sustained similes that are known as Epic Similes; the same kind of device may occur in prose:

'Too generally the very attainment of any deep repose seemed as if mechanically linked to some fatal necessity of self-interruption. It was as though a cup were gradually filled by the sleepy overflow of some natural fountain, the fulness of the cup expressing symbolically the completeness of the rest: but then, in the next stage of the process, it seemed as though the rush and torrent-like babbling of the redundant waters, when running over from every part of the cup, interrupted the slumber which in their earlier stage of silent gathering they had so naturally produced.'

DE QUINCEY: *Confessions of an English Opium-Eater*

3. *Analogy*

In English we need some word for a figure of speech that seems to be half-way between a simile and a metaphor; perhaps Analogy will serve. This is a comparison in which some acknowledgment is made, but, as it were, indirectly; perhaps two examples will make this distinction clear.

'I do not believe that Rafael taught Mich. Angelo, or that Mich. Angelo taught Rafael, any more than I believe that the Rose teaches the Lilly how to grow, or the Apple tree teaches the Pear tree how to bear Fruit.'

WILLIAM BLAKE.
(In a marginal note on Reynold's Discourses)

'Let me make use of an illustration. In the combination of colours, very different results are produced by a difference in their selection and juxtaposition; red, green, and white change their shades, according to the contrast to which they are submitted. And, in like manner, the drift and meaning of a branch of knowledge varies with the company in which it is introduced to the student.'

NEWMAN: *The Scope and Nature of University Education*

Analogy may extend over several pages. Its proper function is to make something clear, but the trick of making something less clear by an analogy that is not really illuminating and only appears to be so is so common that in logic it is given the special name of *false analogy*.[1]

4. *Personification*

This is another very common figure of speech and is really a special kind of metaphor, in which some object, place or abstract idea is turned into a person with human attributes so that we can talk about it more intelligibly or vigorously. This too is often used in common speech: 'America is concerned about the Far Eastern question' or 'Charity seeketh not its own' and the personification of God as a male figure[2] has led to much eccentricity of speech and theology.

'The old houses can always chatter of what has fallen from them by indiscreet neglect or foolish care, and all must regret the blotting of the little unnecessary trifles that were part of their nobility, like the grassy spaces between the garden wall and the public road, where the fowls paraded, and the ivy was plaited with periwinkle to the edge of the gutter. These

[1] The reader will find a very good account of false analogy in Susan Stebbing's *Thinking to Some Purpose*.

[2] I refer, of course, to primitive anthropomorphism, not to the doctrine of the Incarnation.

middle-aged houses make no such appeal. They gibber in premature senility, between tragedy and comedy.'

EDWARD THOMAS: *Rain*

'But the iniquity of oblivion *blindly scattereth her Poppy*, and deals with the memory of men without distinction to merit of perpetuity.'

SIR THOMAS BROWNE: *Urn Burial*

5. *Metonymy*

This means 'change of name' and is used when we speak of 'Whitehall' meaning the Civil Service, or 'Bacchus and Venus' for drinking and making love.

6. *Synecdoche*

This is a special kind of metonymy, in which part of something is used to symbolize the whole, as in 'All *hands* on deck!' The hands of the sailors are important for the moment, though the rest of each sailor will have to come as well.

Neither of these figures is very important in English.

7. *Euphemism*

This is usually a form of Metonymy or Metaphor, but the figure is often defined by its purpose rather than by the technique used. It is the device of using a substituted expression to disguise some fact or idea that is distressing, offensive, or embarrassing. We say someone is 'tight' or 'tiddly' when we mean 'drunk'; a friend may have 'passed away' or be leading a 'wild' life. Euphemism is rather overdone in English; it is sometimes desirable to avoid causing pain, but can become mealy-mouthed and silly. Sensible people will be guided by the society they are in; some expressions may be acceptable in the family circle or private conversation, but not in a public lecture, in the pub but not in the pulpit. It is as rude to use euphemisms that other people do not understand, and so perhaps cause them embarrassment, as to use language that is too crude for the occasion.

8. *Prolepsis*

In textbooks we nearly always find as the example of this figure Keats' famous lines:

> 'So the two brothers and their *murdered* man
> Rode past fair Florence.'

Isabella

and thus we are led to think that the figure is rare. It is the device by which we refer to something as done before the intended action is completed. 'He struck his enemy *dead*' is really a prolepsis; so is 'We are hoping to take some *prisoners*', for they are not prisoners till they have been taken. However, the figure seldom has any emotional power in English.

9. *Transferred Epithet*

This is a device we often read without noticing; an adjective properly attached to one word is transferred to another, as when Pope speaks of an arrow as 'the flying wound' when it is really the arrow that flies. This figure seldom has powerful emotional effects and is not common in prose.

10. *Syllepsis*

A word is used to cover two senses at once; the result is formally grammatical, but odd. This too is not an important figure and is generally used facetiously. 'She helped me to jelly with a silver spoon and a sweet smile.'

11. *Zeugma.*

Another of those figures for which we learn the name because we have the name; it is of no real importance in English rhetoric. One word is connected with two words or groups of words and a second word must be assumed to make the sense strictly accurate.

'We sat down and ate a little bread and wine.' (People drink wine.)

12. *Inversion*

Turning round the order of words so as to give special emphasis to one word or group. This is commoner in poetry than in prose, but can also be very effective in prose both for the rhythm and for the sense.

'In paradise, the fruits were ripe, the first minute, and in heaven it is alwaies Autumne, his mercies are ever at their maturity.'

JOHN DONNE: *LXXX Sermons* (Sermon II)

('It is always autumn in heaven' would be correct enough, but how much it would lose!)

13. *Hyperbole*

Deliberate exaggeration for the sake of effect. Most of us use hyperbole every day without realizing that we are doing it, in such expressions as 'I nearly died of laughing'. 'Thank you a thousand times' or 'You could have knocked me down with a feather'. The device is commoner in verse than in serious prose, but is also fairly common in prose, though not at the present day.

'Like other amphibious animals, we must come occasionally on shore: but the water is more properly our element, and in it, like them, as we find our greatest security, so we exert our greatest force.'

BOLINGBROKE: *The Idea of a Patriot King*

(The British are not, after all, fish.)

'The whole house was constantly in a state of inundation, under the discipline of mops and brooms and scrubbing-brushes; and the good housewives of those days were a kind of amphibious animal, delighting exceedingly to be dabbling in water—insomuch that a historian of the day gravely tells us, that many of his townswomen grew to have webbed fingers like unto a duck; and some of them, he had little doubt, could the matter be examined into, would be found to have the tails of mermaids—but this I look upon to be a mere sport of fancy, or what is worse, a wilful misrepresentation.'

WASHINGTON IRVING: *A History of New York*

'The blue bird carries the sky on his back.'

THOREAU

14. *Litotes, Meiosis* or *Understatement*

This device is more congenial to the modern Englishman than hyperbole, and is often used, perhaps rather more consciously than some figures, in ordinary speech. A lecturer to a Services audience told his pupils that a certain mistake might lead to a crash in the sea and concluded, 'It isn't very funny'. Most people in situations of continuous strain are apt to use understatement as a form of self-protection.

'I hope it is no very cynical asperity not to confess obligations where no benefit has been received.'

SAMUEL JOHNSON
(in his famous letter to Lord Chesterfield)

And at the same time there arose no small stir about that way'
Acts of the Apostles, 19, 23

(That is, there arose a tremendous stir.)

Meiosis sometimes overlaps Euphemism, as in such defensive expressions as 'He stopped a bullet last night, poor chap'.

15. *Pun.* (The early critics called this Paronomasia)

A play upon words, usually for comic effect, though there are serious puns in such writers as Shakespeare and Donne. The pun is regarded as vulgar because many bad ones are made, and a person who is always making puns is a social nuisance; but a good pun in the right place may be amusing and clever.

'I might suspect his thermometer (as indeed I did, for we Harvard men are apt to think ill of any graduation but our own); but it was a poor consolation. The fact remained that his herald Mercury, standing tiptoe, could look down on mine. I seem to glimpse something of this familiar weakness in Mr. White. He, too, has shared in these mercurial triumphs and defeats.'

JAMES RUSSELL LOWELL: *My Study Windows*

(Three puns in four sentences—but they are all good ones.)

16. *Alliteration*

The use of two or more words, near to each other, beginning with the same letter. This is much more common in verse than in prose and can be overdone in both, especially in prose; but it is agreeable in small quantities.

'It is he that puts into a man all the wisdom of the world without speaking a word. . . . ("He" is Death.)

SIR WALTER RALEIGH: *A History of the World*

Alliteration occurs in many popular phrases.

17. *Assonance*

Similarity of vowel sounds. This is commoner in poetry than in prose and can be a fault if it is too obvious in prose.

18. *Onomatopoeia*

Language in which the actual sound of the words suggests their meaning.

'The bees are buzzing and humming with great zest; the doves are cooing; and the children chatter as they clatter downstairs to come and dabble in the cool stream.'

It is more important in poetry than in prose, but can be important in prose.[1]

19. Irony

This is one of the most important figures of speech in English and one of the hardest to define accurately. The stock definition 'saying one thing while meaning another' is too wide; it is not ironical, merely civil, to say 'I am so glad to see you' when we are thinking, 'I wish you had chosen a more convenient time to call'. Irony is saying one thing while meaning another, not in the sense of untruth or of the kind of double meaning found in pun and metaphor, but in the sense of meaning something different to someone else who hears the speech and is intelligent enough to see the further meaning, or equipped with the knowledge to do so. The tone of voice or form of words shows what is intended. Meiosis may often be a form of irony. It is a highly sophisticated device and is found in many of the greatest writers. Fielding's *Jonathan Wild*, Swift's *A Modest Proposal* and Defoe's *The Shortest Way with the Dissenters* are examples of whole books which are ironical.

'But dismissing Mrs. Slipslop was a point not so easily to be resolved upon: she had the utmost tenderness for her reputation, as she knew on that depended many of the most valuable blessings of life; particularly cards, making curt'sies in public places, and, above all, the pleasure of demolishing the reputa-

---

[1] I have devoted a whole chapter to this device in my *The Anatomy of Poetry*.

tions of others, in which innocent amusement she had an extraordinary delight.'

FIELDING: Joseph Andrews

Here Fielding is speaking half through Lady Booby's mouth directly, half in his own person, ironically. His phrasing makes it clear that he himself thinks the pleasures Lady Booby regards as supreme are trivial and the destruction of reputations far from innocent.

Dramatic irony is the special kind of irony often found in a play, an irony of situation in which what is said on the stage means more to the audience than to the person who says it, or hears it. The Greek tragedies and *Macbeth* are full of dramatic irony. A living English writer who is a constant user of irony in his prose and dramas, irony both of language and of situation, is Somerset Maugham. Thomas Hardy made very great use of ironies of situation and even called a book of short stories *Life's Little Ironies*. Irony is favoured by the French even more than by the British.

Irony, which gives pleasure, relief or stimulus and is a friendly device, seeming to take people into the writer's or speaker's confidence, should not be confused with sarcasm, which needs a victim, is used for the deliberate infliction of pain and is not a weapon for civilized people.

20. *Antithesis*

Emphasizing ideas by placing them in clear, direct contrast. This device may consist of a single sentence, or a pair of words or phrases in a sentence; or it may extend over several paragraphs. The Book of Proverbs is full of antitheses.

'Reading furnishes the mind only with materials of knowledge; it is thinking makes what we read ours.'

JOHN LOCKE: Of the Conduct of the Understanding

'When a servant is called before his master, he does not come with an expectation to hear himself rated for some trivial fault, threatened to be stripped, or used with any other unbecoming language, which mean masters often give to worthy servants; but it is often to know, what road he took that he came so readily back according to order: whether he passed by such a ground; if the old man who rents it is in good health; or whether he gave Sir Roger's love to him, or the like.

A man who preserves a respect founded on his benevolence to his dependants, lives rather like a prince than as a master in his family: his orders are received as favours rather than as duties; and the distinction of approaching him is part of the reward for executing what is commanded by him.'

STEELE: *The Spectator*

21. *Epigram*

A short pointed saying that may be more emphatic than a whole paragraph on the subject would be. An Aphorism is much the same thing, but does not necessarily have the touch of wit we find in an Epigram. Most proverbs are epigrams. Examples of prose epigrams will be found in large quantities in the essays of Francis Bacon and the stories and plays of Oscar Wilde.

22. *Paradox*

This is generally epigrammatic in form and implies a strong antithesis, it is a statement that on a first hearing sounds self-contradictory. It can be a very good device for provoking people to think about something afresh, and was much used for this purpose by G. K. Chesterton.

'Truth makes the greatest libel.'

HAZLITT: *On Wit and Humour*

'Nothing is so much to be feared as fear. Atheism may comparatively be popular with God himself.'

THOREAU

23. *Oxymoron*

This is a paradox compressed into very few words. As a highly concentrated device, it is more suited to poetry:

> 'I could have been
> A traitor then, a glorious, happy traitor. . . .'

DRYDEN: *All for Love*

> 'Thou pure impiety and impious purity!'

SHAKESPEARE: *Much Ado about Nothing*

It is, however, sometimes used in prose, in such phrases as 'an open secret' or 'the wisest fool in Christendom'.

24. *Repetition*

It is natural and usual, in common speech, to repeat things for emphasis or emotional effect. In the minute subdivisions of rhetorical devices used in the sixteenth-century critical books, repetition was divided into many classes. Abraham Fraunce speaks of *Epizeuxis* or *Palilogia*—the simple repetition of words or phrases in the same form; *Anadiplosis*—that kind of repetition in which the last words of one sentence or phrase are repeated at the beginning of the next; *Anaphora*—the repetition of words or phrases at the beginning of several sentences; *Epistrophe*—the repetition of words or phrases at the ends of sentences or shorter groups; *Symploce*—repetition at both the beginning and end of a sentence; *Epanalepsis*—the same word or phrase repeated at the end and the beginning of the same sentence; *Epanodos*—the same word or phrase repeated at the bginning and middle or middle and end of a sentence; *Polyoptoton*—the use of a word in several of its grammatical forms. Here are some of Abraham Fraunce's examples (with modernized spelling):

'The time is changed, my lute, the time is changed.'

'O stealing time, the subject of delay,
Delay the rack of unrefrain'd desire,
What strange design hast thou my hopes to stay?
My hopes which do but to mine own aspire?'

'Old age is wise, and full of constant truth,
Old age well stayed from ranging humours lives,
Old age hath knowen, whatever was in youth,
Old age o'ercome the greater honour gives.'

'O no, he can not be good, that knows not why he is good,
but stands so far good, as his fortune may keep him unassailed.'

'Such was as then the estate of this Duke, as it was no time
by direct means to seek her, and such was the estate of his
captive will, as he could delay no time of seeking her.'

'The thoughts are but overflowings of the mind, and the
tongue is but a servant of the thoughts.'

'Hear you this soul-invading voice, and count it but a voice?'

'Thou art of blood, joy not to make things bleed:
Thou fearest death, think they are loath to die.'

All these examples are taken from the works of Sir Philip
Sidney. For all ordinary purposes the term Repetition may
be used to cover all these. The type of repetition I have called
fugue is more important in English than these echo-tricks.

25. *Aposiopesis*

The reader who has difficulty with the spelling of this word may prefer *Rhetorical Reticence*. This is the trick of suddenly breaking off a sentence, leaving something unsaid that the hearer or reader can add. 'Well, I'll be . . .' is an example of this in common speech. This is from the description of the death of two lovers in a fire:

'He catches her in his arms. The fire surrounds them while— I cannot go on.'

STEELE: The Tatler

It will be realized that this can be a good way to touch the heart, as here, or to achieve a comic or threatening effect; it is also a good way for an inferior writer to shirk a piece of description for which he lacks the skill.

26. *Rhetorical Question*

A question that assumes its own answer. 'What is man, that thou art mindful of him?' implies 'Nothing important'. This device is often effective in great oratory and also in the cruel sarcastic verbal bullying of children sometimes practised by teachers who are not fit for their job. It has an obvious antidote, when used unscrupulously, in the wrong answer. 'Are you without all respect for me?' 'Yes, Sir.'

27. *Apostrophe*

Speaking to a person or abstract quality, when not present, as if they were; this is usually an interruption of a speech.

'Waters of Sir Hugh Middleton—what a spark you were like to have extinguished for ever! Your salubrious streams to this City, for now near two centuries, would hardly have atoned for what you were in a moment washing away. Mockery of a river—liquid artifice—wretched conduit! henceforth rank with canals, and sluggish aqueducts.'

CHARLES LAMB: Amicus redivivus

'There was Purcell,[1] who could never conquer till all seemed over with him. There was—what! shall I name thee last? ay, why not? I believe that thou art the last of all that strong family still above the sod, where mayest thou long continue—true piece of English stuff, Tom Bedford, sharp as winter, kind as spring.'

GEORGE BORROW: Lavengro

28. Climax

The arrangement of words, ideas and so on in order of increasing importance.

'What is become of my rare jewels, my rich array, my sumptuous fare, my waiting servants, my many friends, and all my vain pleasures: my pleasure is banished by displeasure, my friends fled like foes, my servants gone, my feasting turned to fasting, my rich array consumed to rags, and my jewels deck out my chiefest enemies.'

Thomas of Reading (anonymous, 1623)

'All that most maddens and torments; all that stirs up the lees of things; all truth with malice in it; all that cracks the sinews and cakes the brain; all the subtle demonisms of life and thought; all evil, to crazy Ahab, were visibly personified, and made practically assailable in Moby Dick.'

HERMAN MELVILLE: Moby Dick

29. Anti-Climax (Sometimes called Bathos)

The arrangement of ideas, words or phrases so that the very last item is less important than those that have gone before. The reader is, as it were, let down with a bump. When this is done accidentally out of carelessness the effect is comic and the passage is spoilt.

'Because one person dropped a cigarette end, three houses

[1] A pugilist, not the composer.

were burned to the ground, a collection of irreplaceable books and curios was destroyed, four people lost their lives and Mrs. Robinson's washing was spoilt by the smoke.'

It may be used deliberately for an ironical purpose.

Here is an interesting passage in which the order of ideas seems like anti-climax, but the actual emotional effect is of climax; in the ironic manner of Fielding, the implication is that the last occurrence, though the least important, would be the most astonishing:

'Suppose a stranger, who entered the chambers of a lawyer, being imagined a client, when the lawyer was preparing his plan for the fee, should pull out a writ against him. Suppose an apothecary, at the door of a chariot containing some great doctor of eminent skill, should, instead of directions to a patient, present him with a potion for himself. Suppose a minister should, instead of a good round sum, treat my Lord ——— or Sir ——— or Esq. ——— with a good broomstick. Suppose a civil companion, or a led captain, should, instead of virtue, and honour, and beauty, and parts, and admiration, thunder vice, and infamy, and ugliness, and folly, and contempt, in his patron's ears. Suppose when a tradesman first carries in his bill, the man of fashion should pay it; or suppose, if he did so, the tradesman should abate what he had overcharged, on the supposition of waiting.'

FIELDING: *Joseph Andrews*

30. *Innuendo*

Hinting at something without actually saying it. We all know the difference between, 'She looks a *nice girl*' and 'She *looks* a nice girl'. Irony may be a form of innuendo.

31. *Periphrasis* or *Circumlocution*

This is seldom desirable. It is the trick of style used by

Polonius and by bad journalists and public speakers, of saying in many words what could be better said in few. Its use in artistic writing is generally for comic effect or euphemism. *Redundancy* is the use of two words where either of them carries the meaning adequately, as in 'grateful thanks' or 'two equal halves'. When the two words are the same part of speech as in 'I am thankful and grateful' it is called *Tautology*. One form of Tautology that can be beautiful, however, is the 'doublet' of a Latin and a Saxon word in a solemn context, which may produce a beautiful rhythm: 'We acknowledge and confess our manifold sins and wickednesses.'

32. *Surprise Ending*

We are waiting for the end of a sentence and it is not what we expected; this may emphasize the point. It is fairly common as a device in English.

'"Bartholomew Fair" is chiefly remarkable for the exhibition of odd humours and tumbler's tricks, and is on that account amusing to read once.'

HAZLITT: *Lectures on the English Comic Writers*

33. *Playful use of Colloquialism*

It is possible to write a piece of prose, especially an essay, in quite a grave and formal style, then suddenly to lighten the atmosphere by some colloquial expression. There is no special name in English for this device. Mr. Churchill's famous 'Some chicken!' is one of the best imaginable examples of this device. In written prose too it usually has a mildly comic effect, or suggests that the writer feels friendly towards the reader. This is probably a colloquialism:

'They say the quickness of repartees in argumentative scenes receives an ornament from the verse. Now what is more unreasonable than to imagine that a man should not only

light upon the wit, but the rhyme too, upon the sudden?
This *nicking* of him who spoke before both in sound and
measure, is so great a happiness, that you must at least suppose
the persons of your play to be born poets. . . .'

DRYDEN: Essay of Dramatic Poesy

34. *Conscious use of Cliché*

I suppose this might be classified as a form of irony. It is
possible to take some expression that everyone takes for
granted and repeats, often as an excuse for not thinking, and
to play with it so as to expose its emptiness or falsity. Here is
an example from a book of political exposition; it is somewhat emotional as compared with the rest of the book, but
very successful as the dramatic climax to a dignified argument:

'Whenever I hear this suggestion that socialism is contrary
to human nature, I want to ask the opposite question: Is
capitalism contrary to human nature? Is it contrary to human
nature to give the highest pay to those who do no work at
all; to give the lowest pay to those who do the heaviest work?
Is it contrary to human nature to pay ninety per cent of the
population so little that they cannot buy enough to keep
themselves in employment? Is it contrary to human nature to
keep several million people permanently idle while they, and
many others, lack the very goods that they ought to be
producing: Is it contrary to human nature deliberately to
destroy food, clothes and many other forms of wealth, in
order to render the production of further wealth profitable
again? Is it contrary to human nature so to arrange things that
the only job on which men can get employment is building
armaments with which to kill each other? Is it contrary to
human nature to send millions of men out to slaughter each
other in order to decide who shall possess the markets of

the world? Is all this contrary to human nature? I think it is.'

JOHN STRACHEY: *Why you should be a Socialist*

The gentle modesty of the last sentence makes the climax more convincing. Cobbett is another writer who is very fond of turning some catch-phrase against his adversary. It is also possible to take some insult or invective hurled at us by an opponent and modify it for our own use.

35. *Quotation*

This is a favourite device with many English writers and may be serious or frivolous. A quotation from some other book may be used in almost any kind of book to add authority to what is said, to express it better than the writer thinks he could or as evidence of something that is under discussion; but as ornament quotation is often a rhetorical device.

Serious Quotation:

'He was one of those Men, *quos vituperare ne inimici quidem possunt, nisi ut simul laudent*; whom his very Enemies could not condemn without commending him at the same time: for he could never have done half that mischief without great parts of Courage, Industry and Judgement.'

EARL OF CLARENDON: *A History of the Rebellion*

'When the Day that he must go hence, was come, many accompanied him to the River side, into which, as he went, he said, *Death, where is thy Sting*? And as he went down deeper, he said, *Grave, where is thy Victory*? So he passed over, and the Trumpets sounded for him on the other side.'

BUNYAN: *The Pilgrim's Progress*

The use of quotation to strengthen an argument or make a passage more elegant, to evoke the strong emotion aroused by the original passage, or even to show learning, is common at all periods where there is previous literature from which to quote; but nowadays it is not unusual to take a quotation that was serious in intent and apply it humorously. This can be very clumsy and irritating, as in many advertisements; better examples may be found in the novels of Dorothy Sayers and in the essays and letters of Charles Lamb.

'He who takes to playing at fives is twice young. He feels neither the past nor future "in the instant". Debts, taxes, domestic treason, foreign levy, nothing can touch him further.'

HAZLITT: *Table-Talk*

36. *Literalism*

This trick is well suited to English as we have so many clichés and familiar idioms. The writer takes a familiar expression and plays with it, taking it in its literal sense instead of in its usual metaphorical sense. This can be irritating and profane when done too often, like the mannerism of a habitual punster, but the trick can be a useful counter-attack to rhetorical devices unskilfully used.[1] It is frequently found in humorous prose passages in Shakespeare and in some of the modern light essayists.

Curtis: All ready; and therefore, I pray thee, news?

Grumio: First, know, my horse is tired; my master and mistress fallen out.

Curtis: How?

Grumio: Out of their saddles into the dirt; and thereby hangs a tale.

Curtis: Let's ha't, good Grumio.

Grumio: (Striking him): There.

Curtis: This is to feel a tale, not to hear a tale.

---

[1] On one occasion I said to a dull class: 'No one has uttered so much as a squeak this morning!' and someone obligingly squeaked.

Grumio: And therefore it is called a sensible tale.

SHAKESPEARE: *The Taming of the Shrew*

The first joke is literalism; the final joke is a pun.

Rhetoric also includes the art of speaking well in the physical sense, and though there is no room here for a discussion of this, one of the first requisites for real eloquence is a voice well trained and well used.

XVII. A WORD ABOUT WRITING PROSE

The truth is that Simple English is no-one's mother tongue.
It has to be worked for.

JACQUES BARZUN: *We Who Teach*

I have already said that the best way to understand the characteristics of a given prose style is to try to imitate it. It is also true that only when we have tried to write competent prose do we appreciate the skill of those who have written great prose. The sheer difficulty of finding the words we want and arranging them in some respectable organization is a strain for years, may be a strain for life. However, we should learn to write as well as we can, not only because this effort adds to our appreciation of genius, but because we all need to write something at times—if only a letter[1] and also because the excitement of creation is or should be an important part of everyone's mental development.

English grammar and idiom are far too complicated and exception-ridden for anyone to learn to use them perfectly by ear alone. Examples of bad grammar and deplorable style may be found in the daily newspapers and in most books—including good books. Much more than correctness is needed to form a really good style. What does the amateur writer of

[1] Let no one dismiss letter-writing as unimportant. Friendships have broken up because people hated writing letters; great offence has been given by ill-worded letters; and letters to the sick and suffering are all that most of us can often do to help them.

prose need to think about in order to write at least a good common style?

First, English grammar and idiom. This can be acquired from books such as L. A. G. Strong's *An Informal English Grammar*, Nesfield's *English Grammar Past and Present*, and C. T. Onion's *An Advanced English Syntax*. (These are in order of increasing difficulty.) For idiom, the dictionary is invaluable; Fowler's *Modern English Usage* and *The King's English* should be possessed by every serious student of English Useful supplements to these, or, in poverty, substitutes for them, are Vallin's *Good English* and *Better English* (very cheap in the Pan Books series) and Sir Ernest Gowers' *Plain Words* and *A Dictionary of Plain Words*. Logan Pearsall Smith's *Words and Idioms* is very interesting reading as an extra. There are dozens of other books on these subjects. A really excellent and eminently readable book which contains this and a great deal more is Eric Partridge's *English—A Course for Human Beings*, which is worth possessing; unfortunately it is such a big book that it is inevitably somewhat costly. F. W. Westaway's *The Teaching of English Grammar*, though intended for the guidance of teachers, might be very helpful to anyone who was bewildered by the Latin terminology.

Secondly, the would-be amateur writer must acquire a large vocabulary. The best word must be found; something rather like it will not do. The sensible use of the dictionary must be learned—Eric Partridge's book contains first-rate guidance on this point—and the study of the dictionary in conjunction with wide reading is the best way to increase our vocabulary. The best dictionary in England is probably the great *New English Dictionary*; as, however, this takes up more room than the *Encyclopaedia Britannica* and costs a small fortune the ordinary student cannot hope to own it. The two-volume *Shorter Oxford Dictionary*, a reduction of this, is excellent, and the still smaller version, *The Concise Oxford*

A Word about writing Prose

Dictionary, is very suitable for all everyday use. There are other good dictionaries, such as Wyld's *Universal English Dictionary*; and old dictionaries such as Johnson's are often interesting and stimulating.

The student should try to become conscious of words and interested in words. Useful stimuli are such books as Ivor Brown's *Book of Words*, *Book of Good Words*, *I Give You my Word*, *Say the Word* and *I Break my Word*, Ernest Weekley's *Words Ancient and Modern*, *Something About Words*, *Words and Names*, *Adjectives and Other Words* and *The Romance of Words*, with Eric Partridge's *Usage and Abusage* and books on slang.

Knowledge is, however, of little value without the third gift of intelligent self-criticism. The student should cultivate the habit of re-reading in order to correct mistakes. A careful study of Alan Hodge's and Robert Graves's formidable book, *The Reader over your Shoulder*, will help at this point. Reading our own prose aloud is a good test, and the writer who lacks confidence should show a piece of work to some friend whose knowledge of English is greater.

A fourth skill to cultivate is some skill in rhythm. Few people can aspire to the beautiful rhythms of the greatest writers; but that is no reason for allowing oneself ugly jingles ('boil it so that the soil will not spoil it', 'legislation for the eradication') clumsy unintended alliterations ('a just judgment on the Jewish problem', 'an educational editorial'), clumsy polysyllables that break the back of the sentence, anti-climaxes of rhythm or ambiguities of rhythm that make the sentence difficult to speak. The length of sentences should be varied, and too many long words should not appear in one sentence.

Lastly, everyone who uses words should try to see that these words are truthful. Absolute truthfulness is unattainable; human life is full of guesswork, prejudice and mistakes; but we should verify information when we can before passing it on; we should write nothing that is intended to mislead; we should try not to mislead by carelessness or false analogies, and we should avoid the kind of untruthfulness that arises from bad English. Errors of punctuation, misplaced participles, misplaced relative and personal pronouns, misplaced 'only's', double negatives, can be pursued with too fierce a pedantry; but these mistakes can cause real embarrassment.

The way to acquire standards in writing is to read. However, such reading should be reasonably discriminating; abundant reading of trash may make our style worse instead of better. We should read good authors and, if possible, good authors from many periods and with many different styles.

XVIII. SUGGESTIONS FOR FURTHER READING

> Don't be sucked in by the su-superior,
> don't swallow the culture bait,
> don't drink, don't get beerier and beerier,
> do learn to discriminate.

D. H. LAWRENCE: Don'ts

WE can acquire a habit of 'escape' reading that is like the craving for drink or drugs and that makes us too sloppy-minded to tackle anything worth reading. We can swallow the 'culture bait' and read a few books it is a matter of prestige to have read, or pretend to read them; we can also read real books in a real way, which is worth doing. Discrimination includes a certain catholicity;[1] there is nothing clever in disliking a book unless we can give a good reason for our dislike, such as that the style is faulty, the story unconvincing or the characters unreal; people who are always saying languidly, 'Oh, I can't read so and so!' are often rather thin-blooded and pretentious. There is no merit in reading a great many books without enjoying them and no merit in having read particular books; in literature there can be no Stakhanovism.

A catholic appetite for literature should include some books other than novels. The ancient idea that novels were a waste of

---

[1] I have recently found that some people think catholicity has something to do with Roman Catholics. Anyone who does not know the distinction between large and small C should consult a dictionary.

time has now, happily, been exploded; nothing that gives real pleasure is a complete waste of time; and the other superstition that novels are corrupters of the young is now heard only when some novel tells the young what they eagerly want to know. We now realize that the novel at its best is a serious art form in which a vivid picture of life can be given, a form from which we can learn much and which may provoke us to think or may nourish sympathy and imagination. However, the novel is not the only kind of prose writing; there are travel books, biographies, autobiographies, letters, diaries, scientific books and other books of information; there are books on many controversial subjects to make us think; there is history and there are the scriptures of the various religions with their amazing likenesses and differences; there are books of humour, fantasy and parody. The reading of informative and speculative works as well as novels broadens the mind, stimulates intelligence and helps us to develop that concentration which we need in order to enjoy the best books to the full. Essays are particularly valuable reading for the person who wishes to acquire a knowledge of prose style, since essays depend much more on their style than any other form of literature.

We sometimes take a dislike to authors we had to study at school. This is a pity. They are usually very good authors; but perhaps we were too young to enjoy them, or had to read too slowly in order to spread a book over a whole term, or studied a book more than any book can bear to be studied except by the specialist. It is worth while returning to such a book later to see if we can enjoy it. Often we can do something with zest when we no longer have to do it under the pressure of authority. Grown-up people often enjoy having baths and going to bed early. Forcible feeding is not renowned for the stimulation of appetite. Yet I would plead that if in your schooldays you were put off literature by dull teaching, you do not lay all the blame on the teacher; it is not always easy to arouse a love of literature with a class of forty children of different abilities and interests and a very limited supply of books.

Practical advice on the development of taste is not easy to give; taste cannot be borrowed from someone else. The first step is probably to read widely in authors generally accepted as good. One way for the ill-informed reader to do this is to take a small history of literature, such as that by Stopford Brooke or the more recent one by Ifor Evans, and to read as many of the books mentioned there as possible. Arnold Bennett's *Literary Taste* contains a very good reading list with practical suggestions for forming one's own library. The books furthest from our own times are usually the most difficult, because of changes of language, so it may be best to work backwards in time, odd as this sounds. The student should also eventually learn what experimental work is being done at present.

Most of the books suggested can be found on the shelves of a local library, and the librarian will gladly procure others. In my experience county branch librarians are amazingly helpful people. The student should also try to build up a personal collection, for re-reading is an important part of reading. The Everyman (Dent) and World's Classics (Oxford University Press) collections are admirable and relatively cheap; Penguin Books and Pan Books are even cheaper and now include a good many 'classics' as well as many of the best modern authors. A number of firms supply second-hand books at low prices and are glad to send catalogues.[1] Second-hand copies

---

[1] There are two kinds of firm specializing in second-hand books. One kind deals in very valuable, rare books and its prices are, naturally, high. Another kind deals in cheap second-hand books. A good firm of the latter kind is Meyer Loshak, Dedham, Colchester, Essex, who do all their business by post. There are other such firms. Book-collecting in the specialist sense is a hobby for the expert who is also rich.

of many of the English classics can be bought at comically low prices on market bookstalls and in small dusty shops. Incidentally, once our friends know that we collect books we acquire a good many as gifts.

The student of literature whose full-time education is over may like to join a W.E.A. class; these are usually very good indeed. Notices about them are probably posted in the public library. A correspondence course may help the person who is out of reach of classes. Local teachers, lecturers and librarians are usually very willing to answer questions and very glad to meet someone who is genuinely interested in literature. The National Book League, 7 Albemarle Street, London, W.1, will answer the queries of members by post or telephone and has a good monthly magazine; it also publishes very good book lists that are available to the general public, though at a higher price than to members. Thus there is no lack of people or organizations who are at the service of people who want to know what to read.

A few anthologies of prose may provide a starting-point. Quiller-Couch's *The Oxford Book of English Prose* and Mark van Doren's *The Oxford Book of American Prose* are excellent and contain much that is not easily found elsewhere as well as most of what might be expected. An *Oxford Book of English Talk* is available. Oxford University Press publish, in the World's Classics, a one-volume anthology, *Selected English Essays*, a one-volume *Selected Modern English Essays*, a second series of these and *English Prose, Narrative, Descriptive and Dramatic*; their five-volume selection, *English Prose*, in chronological order, is admirable. Pelican Books, a great standby for the student who is short of money, publish a good *A Book of English Essays* (edited by W. E. Williams), both the delightful *Common Reader* books by Virginia Woolf and James Aitken's anthologies *English Letters of the Eighteenth Century* and *English Letters of the Nineteenth Century*.

Suggestions for further reading

For contemporary short stories well above the average magazine level, the monthly *Argosy* can be recommended.

The student should not forget to read the dramatic prose of Shakespeare and Bernard Shaw, and it is impossible to appreciate English literature without a good knowledge of the Bible.

It is possible to read too many books about books and too few real books, but the following may be of interest as well as the books mentioned in the previous chapter: Herbert Read: *English Prose Style* extremely interesting and stimulating and illustrated with a large number of long extracts; George Saintsbury: *A History of English Prose Rhythm* is heavy reading for the non-specialist, but worth the effort and the only conveniently available book on the subject at all; Paull Franklin Baum: *The Other Harmony of Prose* is an advanced book with very good examples, an excellent book with which to follow Saintsbury; but it is not for the beginner; L. A. G. Strong: *English for Pleasure*; E. Greening Lamborn: *The Rudiments of Criticism*; and F. H. Pritchard: *Training in Literary Appreciation* are three small books that may be useful to the inexperienced student.

INDEX

Index

Index

Index

186

Index

Index

Index

Index